THE GLOW EFFECT

*Reignite Your Lust for Life to
Feel Alive Again and Inspire Others*

SAREN STIEGEL

ACKNOWLEDGEMENTS

All books are a collaborative effort, and this one is no exception.
In fact, the best part of this book is the feedback, challenges, design
and love infused herein by the community. My deepest gratitude to
you, my fantastic glow-getters near and far. You're my "why."

A big thank you to Jessica Pierce and Jill Brown for the initial
editing of a book that was overflowing and messy with information.
You believed in the words and the result is stunning.

My heartfelt appreciation to Roy Dequina, without whom the vision,
positioning, design and execution would not have been possible.
I'm forever grateful.

So much gratitude to my family for giving me the fuel, education,
and love (with a huge sprinkle of patience) to produce these words.
How did I get so lucky to be born into this crew!?

And the biggest thank you goes to my mother for not only doing
the last brilliant read-through and catching "chalk" vs. "chock", but
also for conversing with me, morning, noon and night, from birth until
present day, on topics of humanity, relationships, purpose, wellness
and light. If there is any or all greatness in me, it's because of you.

TABLE OF CONTENTS

"Don't you know yet?
It's your light that lights the world."

— *Rumi*

INTRODUCTION | G(L)OING INWARD

One thing I knew for sure: something was off. I was bleak, bitter even, causing people to run in the other direction. At twenty-seven years old, I was ready to retire. I dreaded the thought of starting over. This can't be all there is, I thought, so I sought out mentors and allies for guidance. I was told in many different ways to stay the course in this role, learn the required lessons, and earn enough to have a foundation for future endeavors. Apparently, I would know when it was time to go.

On Friday, April 19, 2013, when my alarm went off, the first thing I did was cry. Paradoxically, I was crying because I was crying: I had a fully functioning body and mind, which afforded me amazing opportunities, yet I was paralyzed by fear, self-doubt, and guilt. Crying for crying was unacceptable. I refused to spend my life like that. Those tears were the call to action I needed to recreate my life. It was time to take responsibility for change. I no longer could blame anyone else for my privileged misery. I could no longer wait for someone else to make my life better. I had to be my own hero.

I never sought out "glow." I never aspired to be a business owner, leader, or writer. I aspired to climb the next rung on the "success ladder." That success ladder wasn't one that I built. The infamous "they," the ever elusive "them," built that ladder. I was following "their" lead. Growth, glow, and connection were not on the ladder. "Survival" was the name of the game, and a huge part of me didn't want to play.

I was moving up that ladder quickly. I had recently finished law school and was a first-year associate at one of Chicago's top family law firms. I had my own office (awesome, despite the lack of windows), a killer

3

wardrobe, gorgeous apartment, and benefits galore. Meanwhile, I was more fearful than ever. It was a proven path—there must be some happy lawyers, right? All I needed was to hit the next rung, gain another few letters after my name or before (i.e. "Mrs."), make more money, and then I'd feel fulfilled, right?

I came to a certain point on the ladder where all the "when-I-have-more-_____ (fill in: money, things, love)" statements no longer applied. On the surface, I had acquired all the trappings of success, but when you looked deeper, there was emptiness. Very little of this life reflected me. Granted, I didn't quite understand who I was at this point, but I knew that this wasn't it. Living someone else's version of success manifested as profound feelings of inadequacy, weekly illnesses and ailments, constant bitchiness, hating myself, overwhelm, exhaustion, feeling stuck, and yearning for other people's lives, just to name a few. That energy transferred onto the people with whom I came into contact. I craved other's approval because self-satisfaction wasn't present. As I sat in my office staring out at the wall, drowning in fear that I would be here for the next five to ten years, I waited for someone, anyone, to rescue me from my misery.

Whether we are aware or not, we ask to be saved quite frequently. We find comfort in the role of the victim: "He did that to me," "It is her fault that I am this way," "If only that occurred, I'd be happy." By projecting blame for our internal state, we're saying that there is something that must happen out there to save us from in here. Indecisiveness, self-doubt, and fear are a few examples that something out there is affecting us internally. In order to glow, we must go inward. Glowing means taking responsibility for your reality by looking inward first.

When I took responsibility for my life, the result was not subtle, and the effect was not limited to me. Every person in my life breathed a sigh of relief when I began anew. I received frequent comments like, "You seem lighter," "Wow, I'm inspired just talking to you," and "You glow." I had a surge of energy, excitement, and radiance that I can't fake. More importantly, as I transformed my life, I gave many people implied permission to own their unique desires, skills, and versions of success.

Some people applaud my courage in leaping off the survival-driven ladder; some people think I'm an idiot. The truth is that the fear of staying in lawyerly life finally outweighed the fear of leaving. Instead of panicking about what I didn't have (a business degree, networking connections, or start-up income), I took my strengths, passions, and willingness to learn and built my version of success. Tony Robbins says it best, *"The quality of your life is directly proportional to the amount of uncertainty that you can comfortably deal with."* Starting a business, living a life based on principles of love and compassion rather than money, completely recreating my life, still freaks me out. When I took responsibility for my life and went inward to discover success on my terms, the universe stepped up to support me. With glow, I attracted brilliant people to assist in the journey: website designers, clients, marketing gurus, spiritual leaders, patent attorneys, copyeditors, inspiring friends, business coaches, and so on. I didn't even know to envision of half of these needs, but the universe brought them my way. The fear hasn't gone away, but by pursuing success on my terms, my response to uncertainty transformed. The result: no longer do I live small, plagued by self-doubt. Now I live big, free and powerfully.

Throughout my education, volunteer work abroad, business development, and coaching, I studied the drive to effect transformation in both the collective and individual realms. I worked with movements in South Africa, Mexico, Nicaragua, and the United States in efforts to raise people up for independence, confidence, equality, love, and community. Yet, such collective movements were just that: an effort. They were a fight, dark, forceful, and manipulative. Many beautiful and eager souls were defeated from attacking darkness with darkness, anger, resentment, litigating—essentially more darkness. On an individual level, without a transformation of perspective, forcing yourself to change or do something different leaves you fatigued. You could read every self-help, weight loss, and efficiency book on the market, but if you're still trying to do better, different, or more/less you're still related to something in the past. You're still operating from a limited worldview. Fighting such darkness with darkness results in fear of failure, starting things but not finishing them, codependence, feeling like you don't deserve things to work, stagnancy, doing the bare minimum to avoid disappointment, paralyzing indecisiveness, and the list goes on. Sound familiar? The Glow Effect is a fundamental personal and societal shift of consciousness. It's a vessel for both affecting and being the change we want to see in the world.

When we're physically injured, our body will compensate for the weakest part. It will carry the brunt in order to endure, so much so we don't even notice that the rest of us is knotted up and fatigued. We can limp along for years with aching hearts, failed potential, and irritations, just mobile enough to survive the day-to-day. When we're fatigued, we tend to make weak decisions. We compromise; not the loving-amenable kind of compromise, but the I'll-stay-small kind of compromise. It's the kind where self-worth seeps out with statements like, "I don't deserve what I want," "I should be more accommodating," "I should be more reasonable/logical," or my favorite glow-killer, "This is as good as it gets."

These statements of a dimmed soul keep you from making powerful decisions. Glowing, alternatively, requires tenacity and faith. You must do the internal work, like meditation, journaling, and getting out of your comfort zone, but you also must keep your spirits high to manifest your vision. It's tough to be radiant when you're fatigued. You glow by daring to go inward. Dare to feel, speak, and act *your* version of success and joy. As a result, your glow brightens. By connecting and living from your center, you can touch, move, and inspire others to confront their own fears, to seek their version of success and joy. This is what I call "The Glow Effect," when your light simultaneously creates AND inspires more light in the world. It is both the name of this transformative movement and the process through which you can create radical success and profound joy on your own terms.

This book is a manual to help anyone frustrated by self-doubt feel powerful and capable. The goal is to develop your strength and confidence to help you go from living small and fearful, to living big and free. The unique advantage of this book is that it offers a step-by-step proven method, developed and tested on real, ambitious, heart-centered women. To be clear, this is not about my glow. It's about letting your light shine, so that you can affect your world. This book is for you if you've ever found ourself wondering, "Why?" "Why isn't this life thing jiving for me?" "Why don't I have the life I've always wanted?" "Why don't I know what I want?" "Why don't any of the books and articles on confidence work?" Then, in your frustration with these unanswered questions, you've stopped asking. You've stopped trying. You resigned yourself to climbing the survival ladder. Your intention is to serve and thrive, but something still feels dark. You've become content with your discontent. With The Glow Effect, you can shift your understanding of discontent, and view it as a signal for growth and contribution. Through this process you will connect with yourself so deeply, you'll transform your world (*the* world) from the inside out.

Only you can make the decision to go inward. The moment-to-moment decision to embrace an inward journey determines a miraculous future and the world's progress. The reason people are not glowing is not because of the way their parents treated them, lack of opportunities, poor education, old age, unattractiveness or weakness. These are excuses and total BS (belief systems). Glow dims when such disempowering stories cloud your perception: when you've decided to see them as REAL reasons for not pursuing your greatness. We've all experienced pain, sometimes on massive and horrific scales. For an easy example, my friend, Alton Logan, wrongly-convicted, proved innocent and freed, said, *"Saren, I can be angry, which means I'm still imprisoned. Or, I can use that energy to move forward and say, 'Now what?'"* After the justice system wrongly took twenty-six years of his life, Alton *decided* to change his path. If he can do it, you can too. Only you can decide to change the story.

Every decision says no or yes to something. Yes, I will change this habit; no, I will not continue with this destructive behavior. In fact, the word "decision" comes from the Latin roots *de* and *caedere*—from and to cut, respectively. Making a true decision means committing to achieving a result, then cutting yourself off from going back on your choice. On the micro level, you decide to get out of bed. That decision moves you. It is a concentration of power. Most people don't acknowledge the giant capacity we have to command a mastery of anything. Decisions determine the actions you take, whom you become, and ultimately your glow. If you don't make a conscious decision as to how you're going to live, you've already made a decision to be directed by your environment instead of shaping your own future. It's not often that you decide to do what's authentic. We rarely decide to go inward and figure out what inspires us. There is nothing you have to do. You don't have to make money. You *decide* to make money. You *decide* to eat. You could decide to starve. Here is the key: with everything that happens, from feelings to Facebook statuses, you decide the meaning you give to such events. With past disappointments, did you decide to move forward or give up? With your family, boss, or BF, do you avoid the difficult questions because you assume how he or she will respond? How about your career: are you sure you know what you're capable of doing and being? These daily decisions—holding yourself to higher standards, choosing love over fear, avoiding assumptions, expanding your awareness instead of letting your environment control you—cultivate glow. With such decisions, you can transform your life in any moment.

You've already constructed a decision-making system for shining or dimming your light. Your system is informed by consciousness (what you're aware of), stories (what things mean), and actions (what you do to create the results you want). These elements move in orbits in and around your being, creating a sphere of either defeat or The Glow Effect. When you think of glow, do you think of a square? It's a round aura, right? As long as you have un-investigated parts of your belief systems, you have blind-spots or "dark corners." Many people think the point of this work is to be stronger, smarter, more relaxed. Sure, those things are possible, too, but ultimately being spherical is key. When life happens (because life will happen regardless of how enlightened you are), how do you bounce back? If you're square, with sharp, dark corners, you'll break. Instead, when you're spherical, you can be well adjusted enough to move through the discomfort and hardship and get brighter from it. Thus, The Glow Effect does not happen linearly. Since I'm writing and you're reading this from left to right, I'll explain sequentially. Yet, your glow happens spherically.

I have broken down this decision-making sphere into the three orbits I mentioned above. The vertical orbit, beneath you to above you, is the dialogue between your habits and your consciousness—this informs your confidence, your response to uncertainty, and your sense of connection.

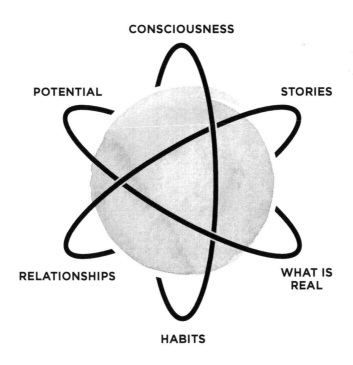

CONSCIOUSNESS

POTENTIAL

STORIES

RELATIONSHIPS

WHAT IS REAL

HABITS

The diagonal orbit to the right signals how you relate to the world—your beliefs, stories, and rules that inform how you relate to yourself, others, and the material world. The diagonal orbit to the left determines your effect—accepting your reality informs how you're inventing your potential. When these orbits rotate, you move yourself and others to create results. As all of these orbits turn, the focus rotates between the dualities: how your habits influence your consciousness and vice versa, how your beliefs and stories inform your relationships and vice versa, and how your current reality manifests your potential. When you tap into your aliveness in these orbits, your sphere of energy changes. The aura around you changes. This is The Glow Effect.

Accordingly, this book is broken into three parts, each part exploring the orbits. In part one, we'll focus on consciousness and habits, exploring wholeness and separation and the daily actions that inform how your awareness creates your reality. In part two, we'll get nitty-gritty with your beliefs, i.e. the values and rules constructing your relationships with health, money, and people. Then in part three, we'll get effect specific—how will you create results? Interlaced throughout this often heady, existential analysis are tools, case studies, and the exposure of my bare-all, glow journey.

The Glow Effect is an inquiry, meditation, and visioning process. I've pulled wisdom from ancient cultures of the East and West, mathematics, spiritual teachings, science, and yogic philosophy. It has no motive, no strings. This process is nothing without your participation. A glow will join any program and enhance it. Any religion—it will enhance it. If you have no religion the glow will affect security and joy. It will eviscerate anything that isn't true for you. It will burn through to the reality that's been waiting to melt away. What is significant about this process is that it allows you to go inside and find your own version of success, happiness, and abundance; to experience what already exists within you, unchanging, immovable, ever-present and always waiting. No teacher is necessary. You're the teacher. You can end your own suffering.

The Glow Effect occurs when you *decide* to strip down your disempowering ego, habits, and beliefs, the illusory barriers limiting your light. It occurs when you become open, aware, and connected. When you glow, it's a vibration that radiates outward. When you glow, you don't have to smile to communicate joy. Your energy communicates light. You're alive. Your vitality is almost palpable. When you glow you have a blissful feeling of detachment, feeling so connected to yourself that nothing could penetrate that energy. Detachment does not mean apathy, carelessness, or passivity—quite the opposite. Detachment is breathing with flow, not being married to outcomes. It's feeling invested in life without expectations. With this stunning power, you magnetize and attract your version of radical success. The "effect" is when your light begins to shift your outer circumstances. You attract the people, places, and experiences necessary to create the life of your dreams. You see that you're not only able to succeed as much as the next person, but your success and joy are contributing to raising vibrations, and are therefore crucial to the success of the world. When you're truly plugged-in, toxic thoughts, people, and past experiences can't stay alive in the light. Either people and things transform or you let them go. A glow is powerful enough to discern all that comes into its periphery. Simply, you must glow, because your life and the lives around you depend on it. The world, the market, your cat, everything and everyone need you to be remarkable. You have a unique light that the world needs. As people around you become inspired to cultivate similar joy, The Glow Effect becomes not just an individual shift, but also a glo(w)bal movement.

A glow exists in each of us—even in cubicles and coffee bars. When you peel back the labels, the job titles, and designer brands, each human being has the capacity for greatness. By going inward and seeking your glow, you liberate your potential to accomplish incredible things. Glowing in this sense means having the courage to recreate your life for yourself and the world. Humans are not only creat*ed*, but we're creat*ive* and creat*ing*. You created your reality, even if you didn't realize you were doing it, even if you forgot that you did it. If you created your life, then you can re-create it. You are not a victim of circumstances. You are a victor over creating new circumstances. If you want to make lots of good stuff happen, that's good for all of us; if you want to earn a living by doing meaningful things, then you're already exceptional. You're already glowing. You are light.

PART
One

Glow Like All Lives
Depend on It

....

VERTICAL ORBIT
Consciousness & Habits

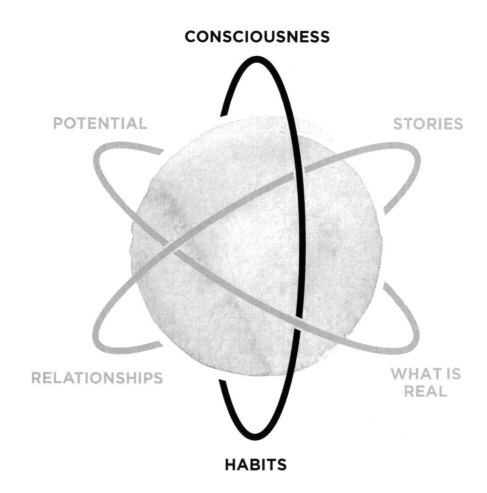

CONSCIOUSNESS

POTENTIAL

STORIES

RELATIONSHIPS

WHAT IS
REAL

HABITS

CHAPTER

One

When life throws you lemons,
do you refuse, make lemonade,
or get hit in the head?

My eyes closed as the wheels began to move the plane backward. I focused on my breath. *What are you afraid of?* I said to myself, *You have been to more dangerous countries. Not to mention, people have made this same trek to lands unknown without your giant travel guide! Chill, darling.* Despite my road-well-traveled pep talk, fear kept bubbling. In fact, throughout that flight to Guatemala; along creaky, school bus rides through El Salvador, Honduras, and Nicaragua; and pretty much every day until I returned back to my English-speaking country, I felt fear. It wasn't mortal-danger fear (although, when I climbed inside volcanoes or night scuba-dived that came up too). It was the culture-shock type of fear. Not only was I baffled by indigenous ways of living; I was shocked by my personal shift in awareness to absorb it all. At the ripe age of 22, I was challenging every assumption of what I thought life was supposed to be. All alone, on a plane to a foreign land, without plans or people to rely on, with nothing but a guidebook and my backpack, everything was drastically out of my comfort zone. In order to make this trek, I had to undergo a transformation of consciousness. I had to break down my traditional ways in order to break through to an expanded way of viewing the world.

It's well-known that most, if not all, of your growth occurs outside of our comfort zone as you learn to deal with the uncertainty. Glowing is determined by your response to this uncertainty. How do you react when growth requires leaving your cozy comforts: do you dive into the abyss, or do you stay rooted? Do you shoot for those big, juicy dreams of travel, love, fame, and fortune, or do you shy away because of the risks involved? There are scarier experiences than a solo-backpacking trip through Central America. For you, moving to a new city, breaking up with a partner, or leaving a comfortable job could be scarier. Instead of fighting darkness and fear, augment your light so that you can see what fear is truly signaling: an opportunity to thrive. To be the most effective, you must be thriving—you must be the change you wish to see. Success and joy aren't things you obtain, like a blouse or a bike. They're experiences that emerge from a new way of being. Before you can create circumstances and experiences (the "effect" of glow), you must be success and joy. You must be light.

"The most important decision we ever make," as Albert Einstein says, *"is whether we live in a friendly universe or a hostile universe."* In that moment on the plane to Guaté, my fear felt as real as any other. I was making a drastic headfirst leap out of my comfort zone. Nevertheless, I decided the universe was for me, not against me. I would see fear as a sign that if an experience were outside of my comfort zone, I would still take part. By shifting my habitual response to fear, by trusting in the universe, I opened myself to new ways of being. It's not that I completely transformed in that second or adopted Honduran, ex-pat cultural practices. Rather, I stopped tensing and retreating at the presence of perceived "otherness" in new cultures, experiences, and ideas. I didn't fret at a late train or a flat tire. Instead, I trusted that the universe brought me these challenges to brighten my glow. My consciousness expanded to see that with infinite ways of being, my concept of "normalcy" was an illusion. Since ways of being are no better or worse than another, the only truth in success, joy, and life is how you define it.

Glowing is a way of being. When you glow, you're the opposite of tense and reactionary. You're quite literally light. You're open and at peace. You're strong and grounded, yet supple and kind. A difference in being begins with your consciousness around two mutually dependent elements: (1) trust in the universe, and (2) trust in yourself.

Before we get to your individual capabilities, let's focus on the universe: do you live in a big supportive universe full of opportunities, loving people and resources? Or is your world narrow and limited where only the fittest survive?

I was raised in a small, conservative town outside of Pittsburgh, Pennsylvania, called Sewickley. It was commonly referred to as "The Sewickley Bubble." Imagine lots of kids running around, country clubs, canopied tree-lined streets, so safe that you can leave your house doors unlocked and keys in your car ignition. This bubble created a lovely illusion of comfort and security. Yet, it was just that: an illusion. Death, rejection, and tragedy were just as likely here as anywhere else. The truth is that we all live in our own bubbles. You walk around thinking about to-do lists or people within your inner circle, maybe observing the trees and sidewalks in your periphery, but other people's concerns are distant. Your bubble is manageable. As human beings we only have a limited capacity, despite travel and experience, to empathize with people outside of our immediate sphere. A sacrifice of power occurs, however, when this consciousness becomes an imaginary, protective barrier that keeps you from connecting to yourself and others.

Glowing requires popping the bubble and breaking down the illusionary barrier, not to be unsafe (although, maybe that's necessary for surrender), but to see that you're always safe. When you pop the bubble of your awareness, you remain spherical, only your sphere of influence and connection expands. Through The Glow Effect process, you push yourself out of your comfort zone and traditional walls in order to reveal your infinite power as a human being. The goal: to find the comfort in the discomfort.

Author and influencer, Marianne Williamson says, *"The Answer (with a capital A) to any question is the state of consciousness in which you simply know the answer."* This is akin to Einstein's formulation: you can't solve a problem from the same logical level it was developed. In order to glow, in order to have the greatest and brightest impact, you must go to an expanded level of awareness, which can be called a 'higher' state of consciousness. If you practice this diligently and go to higher states of consciousness every time you hit a challenge, your fear dissolves effortlessly. As Williamson paraphrased from *A Course in Miracles*, *"The issue isn't that we don't know what [the universe] is telling us; the issue is that we don't like what we're hearing."* When you strive for glow, paradoxically, you stop striving. You recognize, understand and quiet fear in order to listen. Then from this higher state of consciousness, you can hear and live bigger.

The first orbit of The Glow Effect is the exploration of this so-called consciousness, the sum total of your thoughts, feelings, and beliefs, and the habits you use to reveal or hide your glow. By raising your consciousness of universal connection, your light illuminates doors opening. You see and attract new things with the universe supporting you. When I say, *"Raise your consciousness,"* it means to become more aware of your role among humanity; literally, raise your awareness up through the following three levels:

> **LEVEL ONE:** Ego consciousness, where your focus is on yourself and your immediate sphere.

> **LEVEL TWO:** Ethnocentric consciousness, where you care about people like you and your cultural groups, i.e. fellow Jews, Chinese, lawyers, Democrats, artists, etc.

> **LEVEL THREE:** Spirit consciousness, where you're aware and loving of all beings regardless of size, shape, religion, political affiliation, or color.

Thus, to be more spiritual simply means to be more loving. When you start this exploration, you have all kinds of expectations. You're looking for solutions to that hunger, that emptiness that's been present for years. The last thing you expect is further introduction to fear. Yet, being love is about knowing fear, looking it right in the eye—not as a way to solve problems, but as an undoing of old ways of seeing, hearing, thinking, feeling, smelling, and living. With every challenge, you are humbled by fear, so that courage must grow.

Spirit consciousness, disguised as fear, kicks your ass into growth. In this way, faith is not blind—faith is visionary. The universe envisions progress, growth. To do so, it is both self-organizing and self-correcting. You know that an embryo will grow into a baby, a seed will grow into a flower, and a spark can ignite into a fire. All beings, plants, animals, and humans, were born to grow and expand. Jungian analyst, James Hillman, called this theory of latent growth, *"Acorn Theory,"* whereby the destiny of an oak tree is imprinted in the acorn from day one. So too, when you are aligned with spirit consciousness, you see that your latent genius is begging to be realized.

The potential drawback is that human beings have this thing called, "free will," i.e. you can decide to refuse growth. When a cell says, *"No, I want to do my own thing,"* it separates and divides from the body's natural flow, creating dis-ease. The difference between an acorn and us is that we can separate from natural intelligence and collective consciousness, causing spiritual malignancy. There is good news: the universe is also self-correcting. Just as the growth process occurs, we're set up with a healing process. When you get a wound, your body works to heal you. When big banks mess up, forces come in to correct the problem. Humans live in an infinite and endless opportunity machine.

The usual question at this point is, "What about starving kids in Africa?" Yes, people are suffering all across the world, so why isn't the universe correcting that? Ultimately, this is caused by a deviation from love in the industrialized nations of the world. Too often, the effect of spiritual malignancy is not on the person who chose it. In order to glow and be spirit consciousness you must continually choose love knowing that everyone everywhere is affected.

Giving up those lower thoughts of ambition in favor of higher thoughts of service will cause a shift on the outside. Ask yourself, "Where am I coming from? Ambition or service?" and a breakthrough will start to occur on the inside. In order to glow and feel success on a deep and authentic level, you must decide to transform your own consciousness.

A common issue of glow-getters is the perception of a lack of opportunities. While you know you're ready to meet someone special or develop that ideal career, you're defeated by a sense of limited possibilities. From that narrow worldview it's easy to act out of fear and scarcity. Thoughts like, "Gotta hold on to this guy, he's the last good one out there!" or "I can't quit my job—what else could I do?" makes you feel stuck and confined. From ego consciousness, there are indeed not enough jobs, men, or money. Your perception is struggle. If you continue to serve this idea of lack, your habits will respond accordingly. You'll have to manage, produce, and control all by your lonesome. It's as if there is only a finite amount of resources that you must grasp and fight over. This ego consciousness encourages you to organize your decisions and choices in a way that maximizes your good while someone else goes without.

When I started The Glow Effect, my greatest asset was expanded consciousness. My measly start-up funds were lovely, a law degree gave me some credibility and a supportive family was invaluable. Yet, those things were limited, as were my skills. I didn't know anything about public relations, business management, search engine optimization, editing film, social media, or graphic design. If I relied on myself to become Super-woman, the do-it-all, one-woman team, I would have dropped fast. Expanded consciousness allowed me to see that every person, experience and idea has genius. With that open-mindedness and desire, I created a team of five, unpaid glow-getters within the first six months I launched. Each exceptional individual flexed his or her skills in support of my vision. Eventually, it expanded into *our* vision. To say that *I* was building a business would have diminished the empowerment I received from tapping into spirit consciousness. Creating a movement together, aligning with the self-organizing and self-correcting universe, felt powerful.

Please understand, having your awareness at a lower level doesn't mean you are bad or flawed. We're trained in the western world to be unabashedly independent and self-serving. It's the massive layers of beliefs, feelings, and habits that keep your consciousness limited. Consider simply what could happen if you peeled away those limiting layers. By raising your awareness of different ways of being, you begin to see light in others. You see opportunities in people and ideas that you never saw before. Then you don't have to be everything to everyone—you can accentuate and magnify your own innate genius. As Danielle LaPorte says, *"Being well-rounded is overrated."* When you admit to your shortcomings, you become accessible to others but more importantly to yourself. Honing in on your strengths makes space for other people to perform, shine, and operate from their true strengths. You then can foster teamwork and collaboration and benefit from other people's greatness. You receive help. You create genuine connections. When you trust in the universe, fear and disconnection can't survive.

Often referred to as *spiritus mundi*, or as the founder of analytical psychology, Carl Jung's term, "collective consciousness," the power of expanded awareness is as real as the laws of gravity—unseeable, but provable. In his book *Power vs. Force, The Hidden Determinants of Human Behavior: An Anatomy of Consciousness*, David Hawkins proves the personal and world benefits of spirit consciousness. In every second, the mind chooses among the millions of pieces of data, correlations, and projections, going beyond conscious understanding. You barely have a say in where you place your focus. Your attraction to things is determined by what Hawkins calls, *"a predominant attractor pattern operating in the individual or in a collective group of minds."* Hawkins measures the frequencies of two main groups of attractor patterns: love and fear. Hawkins discovered that love, peace, and happiness have a profoundly higher frequency than hate, fear, and pride. Said in another way, selfless, community-driven intentions create infinitely more power than selfish, independent endeavors. While you operate singularly, your state of consciousness, fear or love, determines both your efficacy and ease.

Your consciousness in love or fear changes the vibration of energy around you. You simultaneously create collective consciousness by your thoughts and feelings, while being influenced by it. If you embody a shameful, fearful, angry level of consciousness, the effect is cumulatively destructive. In quite a literal sense, when you're struggling, your family and friends feel it, whether they know it or not. Their communities then experience the vibration when their energy is altered. The ripple effect spans outward. In a metaphysical sense your vibration, high or low, is felt by all regardless of their physical proximity. Have you ever felt connected to someone far away, a loved one perhaps, and known when they're experiencing pain? Or have you randomly thought about someone and then they get in touch with you? This is tuning into vibration. This is the power of the collective unconscious, both your source and your effect. The Glow Effect highlights that as a part of the collective you must not only raise your frequency for your own happiness, but also for general well-being. In other words, you're both drawn to and shaping love and light. You can align with this consciousness for empowerment or individually attempt the same feats by force. You can feel connected and powerful or distant and frustrated. You have a choice.

Let me be clear: power from the collective is not to exploit, dominate, or control others. Power is the capacity to manifest, give, influence, and reveal. When you've connected with this power, your mind is clear, your emotions are at peace and you're healthy and vital. Your relationships and work express the genius of who you are. When you access the vast power of spirit consciousness, you are generous, compassionate and coopera- tive. You glow. I'm not saying, however, that you must sacrifice, that you must give when it depletes you. Nor should you do it all by yourself. The key is that you must give from abundance. You must cultivate so much love that you can give, give, give, because you have more than your little heart desires. Giving from abundance creates more abundance. Giving from lack creates more lack. Let's cultivate the consciousness, habits, and beliefs that create a daily reverence for what is, while catapulting you into your potential. In doing so, you'll change your world.

When not glowing and connected, we operate as individual beings, separate and finite, unrelated to the collective. During your commute, do you look up from your phone to talk to people? Do you drive by people waiting for the bus? Is your door open to your neighbors? According to the media, this is an evil world. Crime and death are daily occurrences. I defended many lawbreakers as a defense attorney in Chicago—I'm aware that there is no shortage of theft, assault, and conspiracy. It's true, you never know what could happen, and, yes, this is uncomfortable. You could believe that all of this divine intelligence is too faulty to rely on. Sure, something big and mighty may exist, but you're ultimately in charge. As a result of this belief, you may perceive that you're not enough. And, you're mostly right. There is only so much you can accomplish as a singular, disconnected person. Hoping for miracles feels out of the question—your survival is all up to *your* intelligence and strength. With such limitation, suffering manifests quite easily. You're at risk with no hope of support.

When your normal state of being is fear, the ego emerges, the small self that disguises itself as you without connection to the whole. The ego is that voice in your head that tells you to be fearful. In terms of consciousness, it keeps your sphere of awareness limited and small. According to *A Course in Miracles*, all fear, suffering, loneliness, frustration, hate, and anger is caused by "one mad thought": separation from the whole. Do you believe that everything that happens supports your highest good? If today, your car crashes, do you believe that your purpose on earth was served? Or do you believe that security is a priority and you must avoid great risk to maintain control? How you answer these questions determines your trust in the universe, trust in yourself, and how bright you glow.

Fear is natural—it is our physical response to uncertainty. In fact, humans have this mechanism in our brains, called the *amygdala*, which triggers blood to rush to extremities when facing real, mortal danger. It's the amygdala that triggers a fight-or-flight response, a.k.a. survival mode. The ego, the voice that is so incredibly fearful of obliteration, always advocates for fear. Fear of death is what drives the ego, and if there is a chance that you could be destroyed, it will give you a reason not to try. The two biggest fears every ego likes to perpetuate are (1) I'm not enough ("I'm not smart enough. I'm not working hard enough. I'm not rich, young, pretty, fast, skinny, or strong enough."), and (2) if I'm not enough, then I won't be loved. Believing your ego's fears can trigger the same biological response as if you were in mortal-danger. In other words, living life listening to ego chatter means living in a fight-or-flight response: tense, contracted, and reactionary. You don't thrive—you survive.

Often, we use the term "ego" to mean arrogant or egotistical. That is one side of the fear spectrum. Indeed, when you feel inadequate, the ego looks for anything to lift you up or bring you down in order to avoid death. Arrogant, grandiose statements, similar to the belittling manifestations of the voice, immediately disconnect you from the collective. For instance, I recall court appearances where my ego attempted to counteract feelings of inadequacy by playing what I named, "The-Better-Bag" game. The rules were as follows: if my purse, briefcase, or bag is better quality, classier, and more expensive than yours, I'm better. Better person? No. Better lawyer? No. Just better. Can you see the flaws in my ego's reasoning? It's a false sense of superiority that separated me from connecting with others. It kept me focused on something that could very well be inversely proportional to someone's character. You could have a sexy bag and still be an a**hole.

When you indulge in the ego's game of not-enough, insecurities get mighty paralyzing. "I better not proceed, for if I do and it's true that I'm not enough, I will fall into the abyss!" Often worse is when you continue to act, but from this lack of worth. This results in acts of force. This uninspired action takes massive amounts of effort. Think of it this way: when you're stressed, anxious, and insecure, how do you act? Perhaps you're mildly productive, but are you effective and creative? When you feel stress and anxiety on a daily basis, producing is utterly exhausting. When your choices originate from such fear, you must force things to happen. Instead of empowered actions, your actions desperately struggle to fill the void.

Living in Los Angeles and working with people in the film industry provides a detailed education in this small consciousness. What allows some to succeed and others to fail? It's not being more talented or beautiful—mostly everyone here is talented and beautiful. What sets people apart is glow, the energy of knowing that rejection and difficulty is not a reflection of you. When you glow, regardless of hardship, rejection, or struggle, you retain the persistence to achieve your dreams. Those who consider friends and colleagues "competition," in contrast, suffer from distrust, fear, and jealously, the repercussions of soul fatigue. With a limited worldview, it's easy to think that if your friend gets a part in a commercial, that's a rejection of your talent. Truth is that you didn't even audition! Does someone else's wealth, talent, or opportunities anger you or make you feel defeated? If so, notice how success in a finite amount can shrink your consciousness. When your consciousness expands and you're aware of connection and creation from *one ever-creating source*, possibilities for success and joy are infinite. Know that opportunities gained from a glow not only feel better, but when that connection is always available, they can be replicated.

I'd like to take a second to discuss "one ever-creating source." It's like throwing the loaded word GOD in there without expecting people to get offended. I could just as easily use the term *Bramha, Shiva, Jehovah, Jesus, Allah,* or *Higher Power.* To those who speak and think strictly, I offer my regrets for any hurt feelings. While I was raised Jewish, I do not subscribe to traditional Judaism. The truth is that I lived many years rejecting any form of God. I chose to rely on intellect, efforting and forcing success and joy by my own will. This whole concept of oneness seemed too woo-woo for my taste. I struggled and feared, dealt with anxiety and the accompanying psychosomatic results. Simply, this way of being didn't feel good. Since tapping into glow and living in spirit consciousness, life is radically easier. I respond to the concept that God does not live in dogmatic scripture or in a distant, sparkly heaven, but breathes through us, as us. I respond to those souls that have voyaged inward to discover their expression of divine, supreme love and returned to give us a detailed, glowing report. When I say "one ever-creating source," I mean that self-correcting and self-organizing power through which you emerge and receive light. This power, call it whatever warms your heart, created us and infuses us with similar, ever-creating power. This is not just the creativity to paint and play piano. This is the creative power to birth ideas, write a legal brief, and manifest a marketing strategy. It is human nature to be creative—to explore different and new facets of humanity. When you are not connected with this flow, as you distance yourself from the light and ever-creating source of your core, glow easily dims.

Thus, spirit consciousness is not about believing in or subscribing to anything. It's having the courage to face up to your fears of what others might think or do. Fear of death is what drives the ego, and if there is a chance that you could be destroyed out there in the world, it will give you a reason not to try. *You*, however, are not that voice. You are not separate or comparable to anyone. You are capable of so much, despite what the ego is telling you. As Eckert Tolle says, *"The key to life is to die before you die and realize that there is no death."* For glow, you must have the courage to die continually.

In order to create the internal shift required for glow, shifting from fear to love, you not only need to trust the universe to support you, you must trust yourself to expand with every loving choice. Like the growth of an embryo to a fetus, it is in your nature to grow. Staying in the ordinary world, in your comfort zone of stagnancy doesn't cut it. Ordinary means that you do all of the things that your culture and family have programmed you to do. You fit in, work hard, play by the rules, fill out your tax forms, get a job, fulfill obligations, retire, deal with old age, and then die. While there is absolutely nothing wrong with this sequence of events, you're reading a book about lusting for life, which means that you haven't completely accepted this fate. In contrast, extraordinary has to do with your soul—that boundless, infinite energy that begs for growth, to fulfill your acorn-like destiny, to be a power for love in the world. Your soul is what connects you to the collective unconscious, the powers of kinesiology and spiritual phenomena. As you occupy this human existence, extraordinary will encompass most of ordinary. You'll pay your bills, play by essential rules, fill out your tax forms, fulfill obligations, but for extraordinary, there is a miraculous shift in consciousness. When you transform your thinking beyond the ordinary, you begin a glowing expansion of awareness.

Becoming more conscious, more loving, leads to both evolutionary and revolutionary growth. As a human you will always evolve, meaning that incremental changes will naturally occur in your life. As a baby you could crawl before you could walk and walk before you could run. This type of growth and expansion occurs in linear, discreet stages in one direction of the timeline. While evolutionary is a degree of change, revolutionary transforms everything. Transformative growth happens beyond the linear. It happens globally, spherically. Take Starbucks—they revolutionized the coffee business. Anyone who follows will be merely evolutionary. Evolutionary is solid and good, but revolutions, that's where the extraordinary, glow-worthy stuff happens. Revolutions happen every day—you don't have to lead a nation to independence (but, by all means, if the spirit moves you, do it!). A revolution, an exponential expansion of consciousness, can be a whole new perspective that changes the way you work, achieve wellness, or thrive in relationships. As Danielle LaPorte describes, *"A revolution is a way of being that becomes a significantly better way of doing."*

I invite you to be receptive to a revolutionary idea. Your entire existence, even when you were in the womb, culturally constructed your "normal," ordinary reality. You have been programmed to believe that you do not possess the intelligence, looks, strength, or personality to live an extraordinary life. So instead of shooting for revolutionary, you seek survival. Tony Robbins calls a version of this "Niagara Syndrome." Imagine life as a river—you jump in without knowing what this river entails and where you want to end up. Soon, you get caught up in the current— current events, fears, location, dramas, and challenges—then, if the river splits, you don't consciously decide which direction to go. Eventually, the rumbling water awakens you—you're 20 feet from Niagara Falls in a boat with no oars, but it's too late to do anything about it. You fall, sometimes emotionally, financially, physically or all of the above. I venture to say that most, if not all, of your current challenges could have been avoided by decisions upstream. To be revolutionary, to glow, means getting out of the river long before you hit the falls. If you sense the falls in your future, however, it's your soul resisting the walls of ordinary. If you've attempted to contain it with rules or obligations, that soul-fatigue is likely manifesting as burnout, overwhelm, and feeling stuck. If you've already hit Niagara, a revolution of spirit also seems appropriate. Glowing is about being revolutionary—breaking down these limitations, creating a radical self-concept whereby your extraordinary self is realized.

"When we quit thinking primarily about ourselves and our own self-preservation," Joseph Campbell says, *"we undergo a truly heroic transformation of consciousness."* In this way, the revolutionary trust in yourself to be a powerful, creative force is heroic. In his book, *A Hero with a Thousand Faces,* Joseph Campbell found that from the depths of African jungles to the huts of the Himalayas to the subdivisions of Nebraska, human beings share the same dilemma: to remain in their comfort zone or plow through fear for the greater good. Though the meat of a hero's journey takes many shapes, the underlying steps are as follows: (1) a person living in the ordinary world, (2) receives a call to adventure, a call to action, (3) she initially refuses the call, (4) she meets a mentor to refocus and prepare her for the journey, (5) setbacks occur as she proceeds down a road of challenges, (6) there is an ordeal, a major

obstacle (often a life or death crisis) where the hero accomplishes the goal, and (7) the hero brings her knowledge back to the ordinary world. Think Neo in *The Matrix*, Dorothy in *The Wizard of Oz*, and Luke Skywalker in *Star Wars*.

Without reading or learning anything else, please take away one thing from Campbell's lifelong exploration: a hero starts in the ordinary world. That is, every seemingly normal person is a potential hero. Just like the acorn is imprinted with the oak tree, your destiny is a heroic expansion of consciousness. Your destiny is to take responsibility for your life. It's an expansion of consciousness so great that you can't help but save yourself and consequently your world. This takes just as much action on your part as it does divine intervention. Also, note that the journey is not flowers and butterflies. To achieve your dreams, prepare yourself for challenges. You must build the risk-taking muscles required to hold such success. The question is whether you'll take the call to action.

In order to motivate yourself out of the ordinary world, your cozy sphere of illusionary safety, and begin the hero's journey, you must recognize the sphere of connection. My guess is that like me and my urge to leave the legal field, you too, hear a voice that urges you back to wholeness in some way. Perhaps it's that voice that keeps you turning these pages. Regardless of the form, releasing a toxic relationship, waking up at the crack of dawn to transform your body, or launching your dream business, geometry shows us that nothing in this world is an accident. Look around you right now and notice the shapes: the circles, lines, maybe even the particles moving in them. You're part of this divine intelligence. With these shapes you are given moment-to-moment glimpses into your subconscious yearnings for connection and growth.

The discovery of the circle, or what I refer to as your sphere of consciousness, is our earliest glimpse into the wholeness. It is the ultimate symbol of oneness. In his book *The Beginner's Guide to*

Constructing the Universe, Michael S. Schneider explores patterns in numbers and shapes, proving our urge for connection.

> *Looking at a circle is like looking into a mirror. We create and respond irresistibly to circles, cylinders, and spheres because we recognize ourselves in them. The message of the shape bypasses our conscious mental circuitry and speaks directly to the quiet intelligence of our deepest being. The circle is a reflection of the world's—and our own—deep perfection, unity, design excellence, wholeness, and divine nature.*

Living spherically, from the symbol through which you emerge, instantly connects you to your source. Every circle is the same—there is only one shape. The size is what varies. In this way, despite the level of your consciousness, each circle you see or create is a profound statement about connectedness. *"Unity always preserves the identity of all it encounters. We might say that 'one' waits quietly within each form without stirring, motionless, never mingling yet supporting all... Everything strives in one way or another toward unity,"* Schneider says. You are always called to oneness. Schneider highlights that these patterns of the universe infiltrate your psyche and urge you back to spirit consciousness. Circles urge you to be more loving.

Schneider takes care to emphasize, however, that nothing, circle or life, can exist without a center around which it revolves. This includes the nucleus of an atom, the heart of the body, the heart of the home, the capital of a nation, and the sun in the solar system. When there is no center, the entire shape collapses. That is, the center of your sphere, the center of The Glow Effect, is you. You, not your parents, your partner, or your government, is responsible for holding your sphere together. You are responsible for being your own hero. Schneider says, *"An idea or conversation is considered 'pointless,' not because it leads nowhere, but because it has no center holding it together."* As much as wholeness and universal support is essential, your glow, your decision to shift and expand your consciousness, is what keeps you empowered.

In fact, your life fails to work when you resist the call back to unity. You lack freedom when you forget that you're ultimately responsible for your own life.

I was trained to grow linearly, vertically: weren't all of us Westerners? The Western education system teaches children by building upon each idea, day-by-day, year-by-year, to eventually create a knowledgeable citizen. I worked hard through my many years of education in prep school, university, and law school to become an attorney. I'm not sure if I was a particularly smart or even a good attorney, but I passed all the requisite stages and exams to hold that title. For many attorneys, the next steps are Senior Associate, Junior Partner, and then Senior Partner. In my narrow worldview, I thought this was a prescribed path. As my consciousness expanded outside of legal realms, I saw that others were taking quite different journeys with a law degree, let alone a high school education. Some were starting businesses, using such experiences as a stepping-stone for other degrees or exploring different professions. My life was evolutionary, at best.

On my twenty-seventh birthday, I was riding in the backseat of my friend's Prius on Santa Monica Boulevard in Los Angeles, California, trying to appreciate every moment away from my Chicago-attorney role. Suddenly I thought about going back to this incremental path and getting yelled at for who-knows-what. Tears began streaming down my face. I was fully aware that my life was privileged up the wazoo. Not only did I have a job, I had an exquisite, highly sought after professional role. That didn't diminish the fact that my job didn't light me up or make me feel like I was giving to the world in the most effective way that I could. I knew other attorneys could do my job WAY better. Because this role was not where I felt connected to the whole, staying at this firm caused an internal tension so destructive that everything suffered. My misery was draining collective power. Was I going hungry? No. Did many people in that firm treat me with respect and love? Absolutely, and I am grateful for those divine souls every day. It just wasn't the right place for me.

Fear kept me stagnant. It kept me blaming the job for my tension. In that Prius moment, I asked the universe, *Can I live like this much longer? What do I do? And, can I do it without a dental plan?* Something changed in that moment, and my intuition spoke up, *Just leap. You will be supported.* Suddenly I trusted myself and the universe enough to start my own personal revolution. The next day in Chicago, when I indeed got yelled at for my LA trip, I began my leap out of the legal world. Prior to this shift, I believed that there were not enough resources to thrive (read: money, opportunities, and love) and that I was not enough. With this quantum leap, I began to see more possibilities. I saw that I no longer had to cling to my job because it was the only thing I could do. Not only is there no scarcity of resources in the world, there is also no scarcity of ideas, energy and creative power in me. This shift was a glimpse into wholeness—when I felt like I was part of this big, powerful universe, I was capable of anything. This shift showed me that I am both *created* by my circumstances and the *creator* of my circumstances. Instead of *re*-creating my life, I would *co*-create my life. With the support of the universe, I could attain Gandhi-like change—I could be the abundance that I want to see in the world.

I'm here to say that you are *not* your ego voice—you are not separate or comparable to anyone. You don't need to reach for value outside yourself. Seek the value internally. Here's the thing: you're already worthy and successful. As the sphere illustrates, our urge towards wholeness guarantees it. You have the universe inside you, urging you back to wholeness. What gets in the way is where you choose to place your focus: how big is your consciousness? Do you take the call to action and expand or refuse and shrink? Worth is not something that you do. You know from our urge for unity that worthiness is who you are. By appreciating unity and creation you can find purpose in leaping out of your comfort zone and lifting up others. Through the consciousness expanding habits that you'll discover in the next chapter, you can trust yourself to take that heroic leap out of your comfort zone. You can reveal your glow.

CHAPTER
Two

A Habitual Glow

I have good news and bad news. Bad news: since you're born with an *amgydala*, fear will not go away. Your light is determined by how you respond to this fear. For glow-getters, people with a hunger for the extraordinary, the good news is that feelings like disappointment, resentment, jealousy, and anger are clear moments showing you where your light has dimmed. *"Fear,"* renowned Buddhist thinker, Pema Chodron says, *"is a natural reaction to moving closer to truth."*

Despite the terrifying clarity, showing you where you're dark and stuck, these fearful moments are messengers of spirit consciousness. They teach you to sit up and lean in when you'd rather collapse and retreat. The universe wants you to be the most glowing you can be. When you sense uncertainty—unless you're in true mortal danger—fear shows you an opportunity for refining your superpowers. Thus, fear isn't a feeling to be avoided. Fear is an ally. It's your biological programming for growth and expansion. Fear is your compass showing you where to go to live your fullest life. Glow-getters keep going, using fear as a compass for growth. If you're not growing and glowing, then you're dying. It's that simple.

The first orbit of your glow sphere is consciousness informing habits and vice versa. When your day-to-day life becomes a place to learn and expand your awareness, you can grow and everyone wins. You're no longer surviving from a place of lack—you're thriving from an ever-growing consciousness. Your consciousness will shift accordingly: you'll serve a reality of wholeness by becoming more creative, regardless of your circumstances. Shifting your survival habits to growth habits allows you to flow. You can take responsibility for your sphere, while goodness flows back to you. You'll experience a level of abundance of which most people never even dream. You grow and glow not because you choose to lean into discomfort one day; you must choose to reveal your light every day. Connecting to oneness transforms your senses, while deciding to embrace glowing habits daily raises you into spirit consciousness.

Glow-getters practice four, mutually dependent habits that allow this expansion of awareness: self-study, service, forgiveness, and manifestation. While there are general processes for each of these habits, the form will be on your terms. The intention is that you embrace glow principles, rather than adopt strict rituals. When you begin to shape these principles into an authentic form that inspires and grows you, you'll glow. Guaranteed.

GLOW HABIT #1: SELF-STUDY

On a Southwest flight back to Chicago, I happily took the first row window seat, put my headphones on and started crafting a playlist for that evening's yoga class. A woman took the aisle seat, and then a very tall gentleman sat in the middle. The woman kindly switched seats with the man to accommodate his long legs. This small gesture was no accident. Even with my headphones on, I sensed her glow. I was now sitting next to Beverly Danusis, author, speaker and more importantly, a radiant being. I proceeded to connect with Beverly until we landed. We felt inspired, and everyone around us felt it. The long-legged gentleman called the seat change *"a crucial event for humanity."* Beverly and I discussed my vision for women, and I explained the details of The Glow Effect—the process, language, and ideas. She stopped me, *"Sweetheart, it's not about what you do. It's about what you be."* In other words, people aren't attracted to The Glow Effect for the things I do. People are attracted because of the gestalt: the whole, the energy. Beverly and I attracted each other not by doing, but by being.

As you explore this consciousness-habit orbit of your sphere, ask not, *What do I do to get the glow?* ask instead *Who do I be?* Then the answer to your glow is perfectly simple: be yourself.

We say this all of the time but what does it even mean? How do you know when you're being it? How in the world does it make us more effective? And Saren, weren't you supposed to give me information that I don't have already? Here's the issue: when you know how to be yourself, meaning that you know your heart, head, and energy, you're going to be as effective as you could be. And aren't we all here to heal the world in some way or another?

This is why self-study is crucial—you must discover your personal definitions and desires for what you want to be moment to moment. Recently, I decided to refine my Clarity and Purpose Program. I spent months interviewing women about their confidence and approaches to self-doubt. One of my intentions was to discover commonalities among the women my program attracted, so I asked a very open-ended question: how would you describe yourself? In staggering results, the answer was, *"I can be many different people, but predominantly I'm X, Y, and Z."* Clearly, it's not a secret that while you have essential qualities, you can choose to be different characters in different contexts. Often, it doesn't mean that you're not being yourself. You're responding to how the world occurs to you. This creates variations on your character.

When I say "occurs" I mean your perspective of the present reality. Take tennis, for instance. In an interview with world-renowned tennis player, Andre Agassi, he described that when he receives a serve, the tennis balls occurs to him as slow as a beach ball. In response to the slow-moving ball, Agassi is able to strategize and position himself for the ideal return swing. Now if a tennis ball were served to me, it would occur to me as faster than a bullet. In response to that insanely fast ball, I'd be lucky to get out of the way quickly enough. My way of being in response to the tennis ball is no more real than Agassi's. How the ball occurs is what's malleable. If I'd like a different response to the tennis ball then I'd first have to identify how the ball is occurring to me.

You spend so much time focusing on what you *don't* want to do or be that you end up creating more of the same. Instead, focus on what you want to be in each second. You can authentically create your ideal version of you, and your doing will respond accordingly.

You tend, however, to start at the doing level. You'll ask, "What do I do in order to be or have that? Why am I doing what I'm doing? What's my purpose?" Try another way of asking these questions: *What do I want to be in this moment? What experience do I want to have? What reality am I trying to create for others?* For example, if you're a social worker, perhaps your goal is to provide relief; if you're an artist, perhaps your goal is more awareness or beauty; or if you're an executive, perhaps your goal is leadership. Before you consider how to do something, whether to get your Ph.D., the perfect workout, or how to talk to your man, don't think about the exact actions or words, what you're going to "do." Focus instead on what you want to "be." This creates a different perspective of reality.

Take a subtler example: we all want to be "healthy." I could detail lots and lots of healthy habits (the "doing" of health) like eating vegetables, exercise, or drinking lots of water. Yet, the what's, when's, and how's of every habit will differ for each of us. For you, maybe running ten miles per day is what allows you to be healthy. For me, I'd rather poke my eye out than run ten miles, which is not so healthy. This is about understanding what you want to "be," i.e. healthy, loving, successful, so you know what daily habits will effect that experience. Rather than just "doing" work, exercise, or your laundry to survive, begin to "be" the experience you want to see. When you change the perspective to how you want to be, the actions and words become clear. Similarly, when you shift to *being* love, instead of *doing* love, the what's, when's, and how's of living your glow will manifest naturally. You will shine when your conscious being brings about your doing.

Once you discover your personal way of being, self-study continues by exploring what that means to you. If you want to create the experience of love, for instance, every situation provides a challenge in being love. Breaking up with a partner or saying "no" to a request could be the most loving action on certain occasions. When you're trying to figure out what actions are aligned with your purpose and you need guidance, the goal is to connect to yourself so that you always know how to find the answer.

Believe it or not, you have the exact wisdom you require in every situation. We have this great depth of knowledge that speaks to every question you wish to answer. My truth may be different from your truth, but it is truth nonetheless. Too often, however, the egoic fears drown out truth. Fear can be so loud that you reach out externally, to friends, substances, Facebook, you name it, to give you the wisdom or a mechanism to avoid the problem altogether. When you take advice that doesn't resonate with how the world occurs to you, resentment, self-hate, and doubt manifest.

Methods of self-study like meditation, yoga, coaching, journaling and therapy provide another option. Going inward for at least a few minutes a day allows the mind to slow and discover your own advice. Not only can you reflect on your thoughts, you can connect with your intuition, otherwise known as your inner guide, Holy Spirit, angels, gut, The Upstairs Team, your crew, etc. Your intuition is your personal source of spirit consciousness—it connects you to universal power. Self-study is the habit to get you there. When you're connected with your intuition you'll always have access to the truth behind the fear.

Recall *Power vs. Force, The Hidden Determinants of Human Behavior: An Anatomy of Consciousness*, where David Hawkins used kinesiology to prove spirit consciousness. When you connect to cosmic forces, you have the ability to instantly determine truth or falsehood. *"Man thinks he lives by virtue of the forces he can control,"* Hawkins describes, *"but in fact, he's governed by power from unrevealed source, power over which he has no control."* In other words, truth, once thought to be subjective, is actually objective Truth. You can discern it when you go inward. Since you have no control, you either connect with Truth and become powerful, or attempt the same feats by force. By connecting to your intuition, you always have access to truth, power, and support greater than any one human being can provide.

When you try to make something happen sans connection, you're communicating with your ego. Your intuition won't ask you to change anything on the outside. Instead it will guide you to change your perspective—it will guide you to go inside. I used to berate myself when I didn't enjoy going to crowded bars. For too long, I thought there was something wrong with me, because I didn't like bumping into people, sticky floors, and yelling conversations. I kept listening to others' advice. Maybe if I wore more make-up, drank more, or stayed out later I would be cured from my grandma-like tendencies. It seemed to make others happy, why didn't it work for me? Indeed, my inner guide was there the whole time, just waiting to be heard. I was seeking some sort of external answer when really the only thing I needed was to listen internally. This is the same voice that tells you when something is off. As I've upped my glow that voice gets deafening when I'm not being authentic. When you can't decipher between your inner guide and your ego voice, the inner guide is likely the less popular, more uncomfortable and difficult choice. At the old age of 25, I grew comfortable with my grandma-like tendencies. I became available to hear why not losing days to a hangover was crucial for fulfilling my purpose. Again, this is my truth. This glowing habit is about discovering what speaks to you.

Once you notice your reactions, move forward to communicating with your intuition. Begin a daily (or many times a day) practice of self-study and communication. A la *A Course in Miracles* ask, "Where would you have me go? What would you have me do? What would you have me say? And to whom?" I like to tack on the question, *"How would you have me live?"* Then sit for five or ten minutes. On the inhale, say, *"I welcome guidance."* On the exhale say, *"I will receive guidance."* This meditation is surrendering to your intuition and spirit consciousness for the answers inside of you. When you connect with your intuition, you will discover the why's and how's of your being and what you must do to create anything your heart desires.

GLOW HABIT #2: BEING AVAILABLE TO SERVE

While I truly want you to live an exquisitely delicious life, we (society-at-large, your community, future generations) *need* you to reclaim your glow. You have been given gifts, skills and superpowers that are uniquely yours. If you don't consciously awaken or utilize these soul-calling traits, not only will you lose out on the benefits, but the world also loses the genius that only you can provide. The call to action from universal consciousness is just as loud as the call from individual consciousness. When you glow, your being and doing will transform accordingly. This is the second half of The Glow Effect mission—the collective need for you to shine. These two parts, the individual and the global need, are not separate. Quite the opposite: in order to glow individually, you need to be and feel part of the whole. When your being is to serve this greater whole, when you realize that you are not only created by the universe, but a creator of the universe, then a glow will manifest.

The Glow Effect isn't just about making you happy. Thousands upon thousands of books have been written on happiness—how to find it, make money with it, be a beginner at it, with the claim that happiness results in positive physical, mental, and emotional fitness. This is not one of those books. Of course, I want you to be radically happy, but I'm asking you to go deeper. I'm asking you to grow and expand your character for the growth of us all. I'm asking you to tap into a well of peace, contribution and connection through service. This is what will fill your life with meaning, rather than just happiness. Notably, it's not just serving that makes you glow. It's being available to serve. When you don't know exactly how to show up, *being available* opens you to extraordinary possibility.

The term 'meaning' captures your entire framework of ideas, thoughts, feelings, and responses in how you perceive, relate to, and encounter life. Meaning is your view of yourself and the world. It is not neutral. Each one of us will have our own purpose. When your meaning contributes to the greater whole, happiness is just one of the many delicious feelings you'll experience. This isn't about discovering the meaning of life, per se. All we know is that your perception of meaning and purpose is what can get you excited for the day. Perhaps your current circumstances are not making you excited. Maybe you hate your job, experienced a trauma or your biological clock is so loud that it keeps you up at night. With such circumstances, finding meaning is your challenge. This is where your glow effect comes in. If you know how you want to be and the experience you seek to create in the world, and you're willing to expand your consciousness to understand the what's, when's, and how's to create the vision, your light will lead you there.

A habitual orientation towards something greater that pulls you out of ego consciousness. In his bestselling 1946 book, *Man's Search for Meaning*, Viktor Frankl concluded that those who found meaning even in the most horrendous circumstances were far more resilient to suffering than those who did not. Frankl, a prominent Jewish psychiatrist and neurologist, not only spent three years in a Nazi concentration camp, but also lost most of his family to the genocide, including his pregnant wife. He writes,

> *When the impossibility of replacing a person is realized, it allows the responsibility that a man has for his existence and its continuance to appear in all its magnitude. A man who becomes conscious of the responsibility he bears toward a human being who affectionately waits for him, or to an unfinished work, will never be able to throw away his life. He knows the 'why' for his existence, and will be able to bear almost any 'how.'*

Two keys of importance here: first, when you fully grasp your unique role in the universe, your effect on the world is transformative. When you know your deeper "why" and must throw off the covers in the morning to fulfill it, then you have access to the realm of infinite joy.

Recent studies have found that the pursuit of happiness is associated with selfish "taking" and that having a sense of meaning is associated with selfless "giving." One study found empty positive emotions—happiness without meaning (like the kind people experience during manic episodes or artificially induced euphoria from alcohol and drugs) are about as good for you as adversity. Happiness is based in time and space, i.e. conditions must participate in achieving that state. Meaning, in contrast, *prepares* your body for adversity. This isn't to say that the source of meaning and happiness cannot overlap. Happiness indeed can emerge from service. The point is that feeling good, moments of euphoric joy, which can be achieved through external sources, is not enough for raising your consciousness. With meaning, regardless of external conditions, you have access to collective power and the well of infinite bliss at any moment.

The second key of importance that Frankl distinguishes is that your contribution need not be Mother-Teresa-like-salvation. It may be raising a child or being there for another "human being who affectionately waits for [you]." In ego consciousness with comparison and judgment, there may be a tendency to say, "My meaning is more important than yours." As Frankl clearly points out, making one person's life a little brighter is valuable beyond measure. A glowing you is your purpose. Once you discover the "why" for your existence, your meaning in this world, the "how" to make it happen is no longer the focus. Gandhi didn't waver when faced with the how of halting British Colonialism. Neo didn't question how to stop The Matrix. Mother Teresa didn't quit when conditions got dismal. Steve Jobs persisted when he was fired from his own company. Your work is not necessarily to know how you'll glow. Your life changes because you create an internal shift. Again, it's not what you do: it's what you be. If you believe that you're here to serve, being open, receptive and willing, even if you don't know how, you will receive the answers.

Perhaps you're already in a career that satisfies a greater need. Simply doing service, however, doesn't create a glow. Are you being the change you want to see? Are you excited to get up in the morning to live your purpose?

I worked with two attorneys, a male and a female, we'll call them John and Jane, who provided almost identical stories. Their stories went something like this: "I help low-income people that are in need of legal services—I got the meaning thing covered. Why then am I resentful, fearful, and unmotivated?" My answer was, "Is this truly your meaning or is it a job?"

When you expand your consciousness and become available to the whole, you recognize, understand and silence discomfort in order to listen. Then, from this higher state of consciousness, you can hear profound wisdom in such powerful feelings. Maybe the answer is to find a different area of law or quit the law altogether. I'm not God or your intuition, so I can't give you the exact answer for what to do (reference Habit #1). All I know is that glowing means to not only serve (read: "do"), but also to be available for service (read: "be"). When you're resentful, fearful, and unmotivated, you're not available; you're not being the change you're working to create. Regardless of the perceived good that you're doing, your misery takes more energy than it gives. You don't have to know or mentally figure out what's keeping you from thriving in service. Just be available to the answer.

"When you're resentful, fearful and unmotivated, you're not available; you're not being the change you're working to create."

For John, his legal career was exactly where he was supposed to be serving for that moment, but he cut himself off to listening. He was overworked, bitter, and selfish because he allowed service to overwhelm his needs. The result was his inability to serve effectively. We worked on balance, spiritual alignment, and inspiration. Again, this is not about serving from depletion. The Glow Effect means serving from abundance.

For Jane, her job wasn't the right fit. She found that although she was incredibly skilled, because the job wasn't making her thrive, someone could do it way better. The Glow Effect allowed an internal shift that attracted the right connections at the right time. By becoming available to change and expanding her awareness of possibility, Jane found a job that six months earlier she didn't even imagine existed.

For years I let others tell me what I could do and who I should be. I spent years coloring inside the lines and feeling limited by what was possible. I feared listening to the signs of what I had to do to affect that experience. The result was crippling. Instead of creating a vision for my future, I'd become complacent with my dreams. I let things happen. I was convinced that I didn't have a *raison d'être*, a reason to be. I just needed to survive. The journey of expanding my consciousness revealed how much myself, and the world, were missing when I kept myself confined. My desire to live on purpose was my soul begging to be heard. I did not want to live by accident as a useless being, but rather aspired to be a valuable member of the world. This was my first lesson in being of service. I wanted and craved what Joseph Campbell explains as *"The privilege of a lifetime is being who you are."*

When I stopped practicing law, I didn't know my exact purpose, my reason for being. I pretended that my existence wasn't an accident until I actually believed it. In other words, I made myself available to serve. Even by faking purpose, my listlessness dissipated. I had energy. My skin cleared. I lost weight. Answers to big questions emerged: What do I want in life? What makes me thrive? Where am I the most effective, while gaining the most joy? Simply being the love and light I wanted to create in the world, regardless of how to do it, allowed the answer to be revealed. One thing was clear: there is a unique gift that only I have. I'm pretty sure that it's not to discover the cure for cancer or the next Apple product, and I'm cool with that. My purpose is simply to be me. When I'm the best version of myself, I create a brighter world. I have a reason to be.

Your purpose is what you say it is. The details of your service to the world will be revealed with this empowering resolve. Being available to serve can transform the feelings of confusion to self-discovery, self-doubt to self-worth, meaninglessness to purpose. This only comes from living *your* truth, not my truth, your mom's truth, the government's truth, or your cat's truth. *Your* truth is the whole point. Rather than a happiness search, let's explore the intersection between your natural abilities (what the universe has granted you) and your passions (what makes you light up like a Christmas tree).

"Your purpose is what you say it is."

For the following, don't pressure yourself to have the answers. Be OK living the questions.

Begin by believing you have a purpose, and then ask:

1. **Create a list:**

   5 things you've done well AND loved doing:
   1.
   2.
   3.
   4.
   5.

   5 moments when you've felt success for something you did:
   1.
   2.
   3.
   4.
   5.

   3 moments when you've sprung into action to problem solve:
   1.
   2.
   3.

   5 skills that come naturally, i.e. listener, interior design, walking, etc.:
   1.
   2.
   3.
   4.
   5.

   5 things that fascinate you—what could you study for a while or read about for hours?
   1.
   2.
   3.
   4.
   5.

2. Daydream: In what ways could you use these gifts so that you can make a contribution?

_____

_____

_____

Don't worry about how—just imagine a day in the life. Entertain the idea that you've been given these talents for a reason. What does that look like?

_____

_____

_____

3. Tap into your spiritual self.
Write down the fears that arise, then consider the possibility that there is a force that wants to help you live your full potential. What would that force say in response?

_____

_____

_____

_____

_____

GLOW HABIT #3: MAKING THE F-WORD PART OF YOUR VOCAB

Dare I say it? FORGIVENESS! There, I said it. I'm talking about the 'f' word in big and small ways: forgiving your parents, forgiving that person who accidentally bumped into you on the street, forgiving your dog for waking you up last night. Most often you struggle to forgive others because you neglect to forgive yourself. You have an internal teacher who gives you an opening, an opportunity in which you can tell yourself, "I am willing to see this differently." That opening is forgiveness in action.

Forgiveness is a healing power always within your grasp. Forgiveness is never a weakness, for it does not mean that you condone behavior. It simply releases you from the burden of separation. Remember those eighties-style weights you could Velcro around your ankles and wrists (my Grandpa's were royal blue)? Think of it this way: with every thought of judgment, anger, blame, and hate, strap on a weight. "My BFF flaked on me last night. Bitch." Throw a ten-pounder onto a wrist. "My father ruined my life—how could I not be angry?" That gets five 80-pounders all along your legs. "Co-worker, Betty, makes my life hell." A ten-pounder for the other wrist. Now, try walking. Or better yet, trying connecting with another person covered in your Velcro attire. You'll never make a real connection with all those weights between you. With forgiveness, you can un-Velcro your burden. Not only is it easier to move through the world, you're free to connect, receive and grow.

Forgiveness is actually a simple idea, but an infinitely complicated practice. It requires compassion and empathy, being able to feel for the other's point of view. Think about it like this: you have a myriad of expectations for life—stories that you use to define the good and the bad. For example, you have expectations for what respect means, how moms and dads are supposed to act, what being a good friend looks like, what work you must do to succeed, how girlfriends should treat their boyfriends, etc. Expectations are ways of being: esoteric ideas that can work to motivate and inspire. As we'll discuss more in Chapter 4, in order to be dynamic and live to your fullest potential, you must set these values high. Clearly, if you're trying to be all of these expectations, being everything to everyone all the time, you'll fall apart. When you set an expectation for yourself or others and it fails to be met, repercussions could spiral you into ego consciousness of hate, frustration, anger, or fear. As we learned in the previous chapter, these lower levels of consciousness weaken you and those around you. That is, when you judge yourself or others for not meeting your defined expectations, you separate yourself from the whole.

Not so long ago, I went through a break-up and spent many meditations processing the pain. My dilemma: should I paste on a smile and act perfect, or can I show my fellow glow-getters that I'm hurting? The underlying issue: can I forgive myself for my humanness, for hurting and failing again? A friend and business coach said, *"Saren, this is your chance to get vulnerable, to get naked, and connect with other glow-getters."* Hmm, well in that case, "No, thank you." Yet, this is what I ask of the world and of myself, to dare and bare: to completely engage in this living thing so that we may risk, create, and grow for the sake of progress and our highest selves. Need I say how much forgiveness this requires? What if I bare all and people think I'm weak, stupid, or a fraud? This is shame. While guilt says, "I did something wrong," shame in all of its self-destructiveness says, "I am wrong." When you identify with a painful circumstance and make it a personal affront, the result is self-destruction. "What if people think this is a reflection of me, that I'm not _____ (fill in: smart, wise, bright, etc.) enough?" Forgiveness releases you from this shame.

As you likely know, you're trained to be perfect. Perfectionism is not the same as striving for excellence, healthy achievement, or growth. Perfectionism is not a shield from shame. Perfectionism does not exist. When you can't reach your expectations, perfectionism sets us up to feel shame, blame, and judgment. You say, "This is my fault. I'm feeling this way because I'm not good enough." If you want freedom from perfection, vulnerability expert, Brené Brown, explains, you must make the long journey from "What will people think?" to "I am enough." You have to forgive your humanness. So here I am, saying loud and proud, *"I experienced pain. I'm human, and that's enough."*

Take note, this issue was not about my ex or our break-up. This was about how I processed pain. Could I forgive my humanness, grow from the experience, and let it go? Could I be spherical and bounce back? The truth is that we all experience pain—it's inevitable. Whether it's losing a job, a person, or your favorite pair of jeans, you experience hurt and rejection of all sorts. In that moment (and series of moments thereafter when you remember the loss) you have a choice: shame yourself or forgive yourself for your humanness.

One of the most difficult parts in forgiveness is the urge to resist reality. In this case, I'd remember the circumstances, then I'd think, *This shouldn't be. Saren, you failed again. You couldn't fix it.* As I would drift into this shameful mindset, I'd experience suffering: a resistance in my mind and body so great that I'd hurt even more. In contrast to pain, suffering is not inevitable: it's optional. Once I began to notice those shameful thoughts (a skill I'll be forever learning through lots of self-study), I'd pause and remind myself, *It is what is. It's not what it should have been, not what it could have been, it is what it is.* With forgiveness and my acceptance of the situation, I'd recognize that I tried for something. I loved and gave myself greatly. I risked and learned a ridiculous amount. With expanded consciousness and my practice of forgiveness, I could trust in the universe that this perceived rejection was redirection.

As Carl Jung said, *"I am not what has happened to me. I'm what I choose to become."* Our willingness to own and engage with life—the baring-all, scary parts of it—determines your growth and purpose. If you spend your life waiting until you're perfect before you get in the ring, you sacrifice opportunities of love, innovation, and connection that may not be recoverable. You squander your precious time and turn your back on your unique contributions to the world. Rather than sitting on the sidelines (or in my pajamas watching *House of Cards*), hurling judgment and criticism, we must dare to engage and let ourselves be seen. This requires constant forgiveness.

Let's be honest, I judge. You judge. We all judge. But there are two types of judgment. First, the discernment kind of judgment is perception. It's the job of everyone in this world to judge. "My hand is too big to fit into the cookie jar." "It is too cold out for flip-flops." "He is too old for diapers." Everything in this world is a judgment, because that is the essence of perception. We require discernment to move through the world. In fact, deepening your discernment muscle with light, allows growth.

The other type of judgment, the separating kind, is where you assign value to behavior. Anytime you assign a "This is good" or "This is bad" to behavior, words, or choice of scrunchy, you block yourself from connective power. Eww, did I just say "scrunchy"? I'm so out of style ← case in point. The subtext is that discerning my love of scrunchies makes my style bad/less/ugly. This is a value judgment. You must discern the type of judgment you're using to prevent separating from the whole.

The reason that you do not go around screaming, *"You suck!"* or other such judgmental outbursts to co-workers, friends, and family is that you would be ostracized. You would separate from the whole instantaneously. You can put yourself in their shoes. You can imagine what someone else is feeling and create that feeling. You take that tactic because you were supported, comforted, and understood in your suffering. That support gives you a model of how to feel for others: it is the basis for wholeness and glow. In contrast, by judging behavior as good or bad, you shrink your consciousness. Forgiveness is the practice of spirit consciousness where you extend your physical senses to see beyond the surface, e.g. *"You're a jerk,"* into who someone really is—*"You're a child of the universe."*

The opposite of forgiveness—value judgment, anger, blame, and hate—do little to affect others. Even when they do create change, the effect on your physical, mental, and spiritual health is greater. Anger, frustration, and resentment are emotions that trigger the *amygdala*, the "fight-or-flight" response, preparing us to defend ourselves physically and psychologically in a conflict. When corresponding to real, dangerous threats, this response could be lifesaving. Too often, however, it pushes your body into overdrive. As soon as you start to get feisty, your muscles tense, your digestive processes slow down, and your adrenal glands begin to produce adrenaline, which alters your hormones. In the long term, and sometimes even the short term, this response weakens your immune system and leads to a variety of health problems such as headaches, digestive problems, insomnia, anxiety, depression, high blood pressure, skin problems, and the list goes on. After the drop in adrenaline, negative emotions like bitterness, hopelessness, futility and overall sadness can manifest. It seems like holding onto a grudge would make you powerful, as the ball is in your court. Ultimately, these destructive effects turn you into the victim. By allowing others' behavior to affect you, plaguing you as the injured party, you're powerless. Forgiveness, instead, releases you and heals all thoughts of separation. As you move into wholeness, power is automatic.

Forgiveness allows you to expand yourself into spirit consciousness, which lifts us all up. Here's the paradox: forgiveness is not exactly part of spirit consciousness. Wait, why then is this a glow habit? By projecting blame, shame, hate, or resentment on yourself or others, you're separating yourself from universal power. This separation is not your natural state. Spirit consciousness, unity and wholeness, is your natural state. Forgiveness is the remedy for separation, but it is not part of the wholeness sphere to begin with. Therefore, while it is glow-worthy to shift into spirit consciousness, forgiveness is a human habit. When you forgive, you heal all thoughts of separation—you tap into glow.

Now that you understand a bit about this f-word, you must activate it.

Start by listing all of the judgments, resentments, shame and blame you're holding against yourself. Go into a stream of consciousness, an uninterrupted flow of thoughts.

_____

_____

_____

_____

Then put the list aside. Sit quietly for 5-10 minutes, and ask your inner guide for forgiveness for all of your self-hate.

Pull out your journal (or the lines below), and write a letter of forgiveness from your inner guide. Start with, "Dearest me, I forgive you for all of the judgments, resentments, shame and blame you're holding against yourself" then see where your inner guide takes you. Again, this is not a doing. It's a way of being. All you can do is surrender to it. Release is of the universe's doing. Activating forgiveness must become such habit that it transforms into a way of living.

Dearest me,
I forgive you for all of the judgments, resentments, shame and blame you're holding against yourself...

_____

_____

_____

_____

_____

_____

_____

_____

_____

_____

Next, begin your 21-Day Forgiveness Journey.

List the people you hold judgments, resentments, shame and blame against. Yes, every single person: the driver that cut you off, your high school boyfriend that broke your heart, me (just in case this book disappoints you), the checkout guy who moved too slowly, and so on. (My list was over five pages. Just saying.)

_____

_____

_____

_____

_____

_____

_____

For the next 21 days, upon waking and going to sleep, place your hand over your list and repeat the following request:

"My inner guide, I ask that forgiveness be activated within me for every person on this list. I bless them and know for them success and happiness. Please heal thoughts of separation and return me to wholeness."

If you feel tension or frustration welling up at any time during the day, repeat this prayer. With this request, you're no longer responsible for *doing* forgiveness. Rather, you surrender to the universe, healing your separation from the whole.

GLOW HABIT #4: MANIFEST YOUR ABUNDANCE

We've discussed self-study (how the world occurs to you), giving (being available to serve) and releasing (forgiveness), all essential for a growth of consciousness. What about receiving? A discussion of spirit consciousness is incomplete without fostering the abundance to make expansion possible. Our modern, western culture tends to simultaneously promote individualism while chastising us for receiving. So too, the spiritual community seems to judge desires, wishes, and dreams of ambition as if they're not as generous to the world. Both the Western and spiritual worldviews seem to create an inadvertent tension: how can you continuously give to the world without receiving energy to do so? This tension prevents you from asking for things you want or even asking for help.

I used to think that it was not spiritual to want money, until I realized how necessary money is to life. As I'll discuss in depth later, money is simply energy. Just as you pay people for the energy they give to you, you must be paid adequately for the energy you give to the world. Without receiving energy in return for your giving (at least in some capacity), you're going to struggle. If you're constantly worried about how to pay your bills, then giving, let alone effective giving, is out of the question.

The fact of the matter is that you cannot give without taking care of yourself first. And, my dearest glow-getter, taking care of your needs cannot be done alone. You are not an island. When you open your consciousness, you begin to see how you're asking for things all of the time. When you ask a taxi driver to take you somewhere, you're asking the universe that the driver will actually take you where you want to go. When you need a carton of milk, you're asking the universe for the cow, the carton production, the grocery store, and the money to purchase it. Since you're asking for things already, wouldn't it be more fun to start asking for what you really want? The practice of manifestation is not about receiving for the sake of consumption. The practice is meant to up your abundance so that you can up the world's vibration.

When spirit consciousness becomes a way of life, giving and receiving are one truth. We tend to think that the giving comes first and the receiving second, as if the receiver is the benefactor of the exchange. According to *A Course in Miracles*, however,

> ...[B]oth giving and receiving [are] seen as different aspects of one Thought whose truth does not depend on which is seen as first, nor which appears to be in second place. Here it is understood that both occur together, that the Thought remain complete. And in this understanding is the base on which all opposites are reconciled, because they are perceived from the same frame of reference which unifies this Thought.

In other words, an exchange, giving and receiving, is just as beneficial to the giver as to the receiver. When both the giver and the receiver are open and willing, a high vibration of love surrounds both of the parties. For example, if someone wants to help you carry your groceries, it may be more gratifying to them to help you than it is for you to receive assistance. If it is part of their journey to assist you, why would you deprive them of giving? Thus, our internal abundance from receiving is ultimately the source of our external abundance. What you receive, not just the services you provide, creates money and any other energy you need to live.

One of the most difficult blocks I overcame was receiving payment for my work. Despite my education, skills, and experience, I felt that if people needed me, I should forego payment in order to help. When I believed that there were only so many pieces of the pie, only a finite amount of money to go around (a.k.a. a scarcity worldview), I'd feel guilty for charging money. As I expanded my consciousness and began to see the wholeness of giving and receiving, I realized that if I'm providing an honorable service, I'm increasing abundance for both of us. Then I took it bigger. I chose to want money not to *get* things (although, I'm a major consumer of green juice), but to *change* things. This is your permission to want: to want big things, to be so full in your life that giving and receiving become one. When you manifest what you want, you can transform the way you create change in the world. You can create anything you want.

Because manifestation is both a science and an art, there are parts that rely on the practical, intellectual knowing and parts that rely on the intuitive, feeling experience. We'll start with the intellectual.

The concept is almost too simple to be believed: you attract reflections of what you are. You're made up of particles. Everything is: every thought, object, emotion, plant and animal are all particles vibrating at different frequencies. If your vibration is at the level of the experience you want, it will come. Even if you don't get the science behind it, attraction will happen anyway.

This attraction principle relies on two things: first, be a vibrational match for the experiences you want. You must cultivate the joy that the experience will bring. To do so, you must differentiate between the experience and the object/person of your desire. For instance, say you want a relationship chock full of love, joy, intellectual stimulation, and other kinds of stimulation. You launch this rocket of desire and attract Beyoncé. Your relationship with Beyoncé goes beyond what you thought a relationship could be. Then something happens—you and Mrs. Carter miscommunicate over the fact that she is married. Per the vibrations, either you or B were not a vibrational match for this awesome relationship. This is not a loss. You gained a clearer vision of the relationship you actually want (one with better communication and without Jay-Z). It's a mistake to think that only Beyoncé holds this relationship experience for you. It's the vibration, the experience that you are really seeking. This works with money, jobs, and weight loss—you want the experience of having lots of money, the experience of being a doctor, the experience of being thin—not necessarily the object of your desire.

Second, attraction relies on being aware of your vibration at all times. On a metaphysical level, anything you ask for has already come to be. You want a new car. Boom! It's done. The car is out there and waiting for you. The challenge is to become the vibration of the you that has that car. Like I said, what you are comes back. If you want a million dollars, but you're constantly saying that you're broke, your vibration is not at the level of your experience in having a million dollars. Many people approach manifestation from a place of "How can I get something to feel better?" Instead, shift the focus to *"How can I feel better and therefore be an energetic match for attracting more greatness into my life?"* When you become the energetic match for the vision you desire, anything is possible.

Manifestation begins with four steps:

First, the absolute, most powerful habit you can practice is gratitude. When you're grateful, consistently recognizing the love that is already in your life, from the air you breathe to your ability to read these words, more glow will come. What you are comes back, so showing love for the prosperity you already have (even if your bank account begs to differ) creates the vibration for more love to come into your life.

Second, take responsibility for what isn't working—clean up whatever you need to clean up. Make a list of wherever you feel lack and ask, *What was my part in creating the problem? Whom do I need to forgive? What remains to be cleaned up?*

Third, allow yourself to want what you want. When you're aligned with your intuition, you're desires are trustworthy. Get really deliberate and specific in your asking. Think of the universe as one giant Amazon.com. When you're not specific, it's like going on Amazon and saying, "Just send me something." Well, of course Amazon doesn't send you anything because there are infinite possibilities. Get clear and specific.

This brings me to the last step: ask for it, and then ask for it again and again and again. Put your attention there continuously. If you want a blender from Amazon.com, you must be consistent with your asking. It's like ordering a green Vitamix, then canceling the order; then re-ordering a red Cuisinart, then canceling. Then you wonder why you're not getting your blender in the mail. Too often, you expect immediate results. Simply focusing on the experience of having what you desire consistently, without questioning yourself, will make it come to pass.

> *"When you become the energetic match for the vision you desire, anything is possible."*

With habitual self-study, being available to serve, forgiveness, and manifesting, you will expand your consciousness. Simultaneously, as your awareness grows, your habits will refine and your glow will brighten. Fear and your response to uncertainty transform as your consciousness and habits shift to love. Glowing isn't about doing—it's a way of being the change, being the brightness that you want to affect in the world. The orbit of this expansion and journey inward will reveal your light. Yet, without investigation into the next orbit, you will unconsciously block your glow...

PART
Two

Put the Past in the Past
and Create the Future

RIGHT DIAGONAL ORBIT
Stories and Relationships

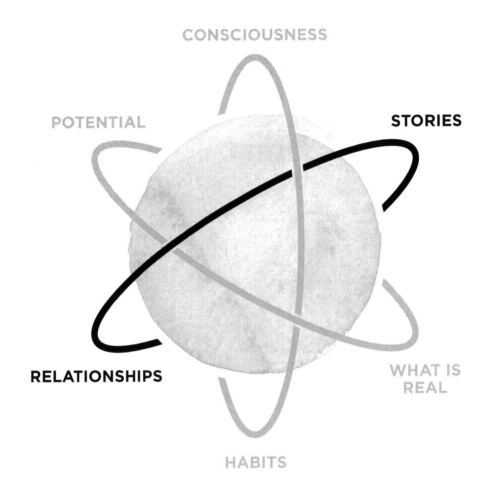

CONSCIOUSNESS

POTENTIAL

STORIES

RELATIONSHIPS

WHAT IS
REAL

HABITS

Once Upon A Time,
There Was A Glowing Story

On a sunny afternoon in Cape Town, South Africa, second semester of my junior year of college, I joined 26 American college kids in an exploration of the country's reconciliation and development. We split into two groups and joined now-grown, child soldiers in an exercise that was used ten years earlier after the abolition of Apartheid. The ex-soldiers gave us markers and giant sheets of paper. We were to draw a life map, highlighting the most pivotal events that shaped us. Thirteen 21-year-olds began carving out whom and why we were what we were— *I'm a stick figure at my family's summer camp in Northern Michigan. This is when I got really drunk at a house party. Here is when my parents bought me a car.*

Then we had to share the maps of our young lives. Lesedi, a 29-year-old, ex-child-soldier, started off: *"About 12 years ago, white, black, colored, and Indian participants, victims of the four, delineated groups during Apartheid, were asked to do this exercise. When people shared their life maps, all were shocked to realize that they weren't so different. We realized that we've all felt pain and loss from this awful history. The killings and tragedies made everyone suffer. Among these small groups, separated from other humans based on skin color, was a connection so immediate and profound, that there was hope for reconciliation."* He continued, *"My story also was complicated. I was recruited as a child soldier at 13, but I resisted. I was sent to Angola and Zimbabwe. When I finally was able to return many years later, my sister had been killed, my father died, and my mother was sick. If I was there, I truly believe things could have been different. Instead, I was killing others. I'm sorry for leaving and killing every day. Murderer was not a role I chose or ever wanted. As hard as it is, I choose daily not to define myself that way.*

I don't fault those whose past was not their choice, but it's how we reconcile and move forward that counts." All eyes in the room welled up with tears.

Oy, how am I ever going to share my map?, I thought.

After Lesedi spoke, others in the group shared stories of death, poverty, joy, and love. Tears kept coming. I was last in the circle and mortified that my life seemed like a cakewalk compared to Lesedi and the crew's. I forced my story out through gulps of air, *"This is nothing compared to any of you, but here I go."* I told of my high school battles with depression, break-ups with boyfriends, family deaths, and my happily married parents. Everyone cried, not because my story was so tragic, but because I too felt pain: this was my story. My pain was just as poignant as the next person's.

Among the lessons learned was a crucial point: each of us has a story, a past that has scarred us and shaped us. You shouldn't feel guilty for not experiencing tragedy as awful as someone else, nor should you feel proud for avoiding the slings and arrows of outrageous fortune. You must value and understand your stories as just that: stories. These are interpretations of circumstances that either empower you for growth or disempower you for separation.

Simply, with every event and happening, there are the cold, hard facts that make it real: someone says or does something. The "story" is the interpretations, meanings, opinions, standards, reasonings, and so on that you attach to that happening. From there you use that story to perceive the world. When you're viewing the world with that specific frame of reference, you'll discover evidence to support your story. You may even enlist others in that perception to assure its truth. This creates the same happenings again. As a result, your story gains even more evidence, you create the events again, and you're caught in a vicious cycle. Suffering emerges when you forget that the interpretation is just a story.

An easy example: I tap your arm. This is what happens. It's fact. You have many choices for how to interpret that. You could say, "Aw, Saren is so sweet. She gave me a love tap." Or you could say, "Saren is so mean. She just hit me." This is the beginning of your story, and you'll now look for evidence to support it. You could go on Facebook, look at my wall, and say, "See? This proves that she is mean." The story repeats. I say, "Hi," but you hear a fake tone and judgment. What happened? I said a word and you interpreted meaning. The story is ingrained.

Every story, yours and mine, begins inside a story that's been written by others. Long before you take your first breath, there's a plot well under way with characters and a setting you did not choose but was chosen for you. This is how culture is created—weaving together stories allows civilization to progress and function. Your beliefs and rules for how life is or should be emerge from the cultural groups you inhabit. You may believe it's normal to say "bless you" when someone sneezes, drink wine with a meal, or get married in a puffy, white dress, but in most cultures, none of that is normal. All of the above is culturally constructed, i.e. none of what you do, think, or speak is inherently true. You project meaning onto everything. The best part about this? Since your stories are culturally and personally created, they can be re-created to serve a new, brighter reality.

A brighter reality is realizing collective genius, the power and purpose we have as human beings. It's no accident that you were born with your mental, emotional, and physical faculties. You can either see your human plight as a selfish endeavor to survive or a collective effort for progress. You have a responsibility to people everywhere to realize your genius. I'm not just talking about Einstein-like genius (although, if you have another take on relativity, please share). I'm talking your unique purpose, your natural abilities colliding with your passions, combined with flourishing relationships—your relationship to yourself, others, and the material world. When you realize your gift to the world, you generate abundance in every element of your life. Cultivating your genius is your responsibility to the world and to yourself.

There is a path to genius, sometimes easily walked, but more often it requires a grand upheaval of your stories. According to author, Gay Hendricks, there are four zones you can occupy:

1. ZONE OF INCOMPETENCE: In this zone, you do things you're not naturally good at doing. Here, it feels like you're beating your head against the wall trying to survive. When you're in this zone, it's easy to feel like you're worthless. (This doesn't mean that you *are* worthless, but if your life doesn't feel meaningful, you *feel* worth so much less.) I equate this zone to my computer ability. I'm the worst at computers, and I have no desire to change that. If I somehow felt that learning beyond Word and Chrome would benefit me, two things would likely happen: (1) I would feel frustrated and depleted constantly, and (2) I would affect people with my computer-illiteracy misery. Thus, I ask for help, and when I'm generously giving to the world from my genius, help always arrives.

2. ZONE OF COMPETENCE: Here, others can do these things just as well. Often, competence, without passion, manifests into chronic fatigue, weight gain, or illness. Your body reacts to this internal knowing that you should be somewhere else. Be careful of doing what you're just "good" at—you may do it for years. You can make room for the things you really excel at by saying no to competence. This was me practicing law. I have some natural skills that work in the legal field, but reading statutes and arguing just do not inspire me. I can force myself to improve these skills (and I did), but ultimately, this isn't where I thrive. Simply surviving in this zone tanked my joy, health, and relationships and that of everyone who dealt with me.

"When you get on your glow, the world— your world—transforms."

3. ZONE OF EXCELLENCE: This is a seductive zone. You can lead a great life here, but an addiction to comfort can keep you stuck. In this zone, you're reliable; you can make a decent living, yet a deep, sacred part of you doesn't light up. You may experience beauty, but it's only in temporary conditions. For me, this is teaching yoga. I love it. I really love it, but when I do it more than once or twice a week, I feel like something is missing. I used to chastise myself for this discontent, until I discovered my...

4. ZONE OF GENIUS: This is where you thrive—it's your glow zone. This is your unique genius that beckons you throughout your life. Blocking these calls to genius is what manifests as illness, insecurity, and relationship conflict. Blocking the calls dims your glow. Your most valuable currency is what comes naturally to you and what you're endlessly passionate about. You must hold firm to what gives you this enthusiasm. In doing so you become the dispenser of glow, where you feel part of something greater. This zone is the expression of your authentic self. When you're on your dime, the goldmine of your genius, you can't help but become more loving and compassionate towards yourself and others, and the world will compensate you accordingly. When you get on your glow, the world—your world—transforms.

Your Zone of Genius is present from day one. James Hillman, (remember the Hillman/self-organizing universe discussion in chapter one?) called this *"Acorn Theory,"* where the destiny of the oak is imprinted in the acorn. Similarly, your genius is imprinted in you. Your purpose, your only purpose from day one of conception, is to be this genius. Glow emanates not only because of what you can create *externally* with your genius—teaching future generations, litigating, or interior design, but also because your genius creates an *internal* experience of what you want to feel in order to fuel more and brighter action.

The right diagonal orbit of your glow-sphere, turning Northeast to Southwest, are the stories you use to interpret your world and your corresponding relationship to your world. Your stories either guide you toward your genius or keep you stuck in the other zones. We always say that children have potential, but adults too are wells of dormant genius. When you're lost inside a chaotic, storied mind, your genius becomes encumbered by junk. You get in your own way. Our work is not to abolish interpretations. Our work is to remind you that in every projection of meaning you have a choice: empowered, glowing thoughts or disempowered, limiting thoughts.

Our task in this chapter is to create a story revolution, an upheaval of unconscious beliefs, so that you may explore your decisions, actions, and ultimately your destiny. Glowing means embracing an ongoing and deepening process of self-discovery, not a quick fix. This inquiry process is a technique that brings to life, from deep within us, an innate aspect of our being. The deeper you go into yourself, the more glowing becomes who you are.

Your life is your message to the world. How you live moment-to-moment determines your life's inspiration, beauty, and effect. When I returned from that trip to South Africa, I was a wreck. I felt so much sadness and anger for the hate enacted throughout our world that I felt immobile. *How do I respond? What's my next decision in how to shape my life?* Just like the culture shock in Central America, I wasn't just stunned— I was forever transformed. I again looked my fear in the face; my stories as to what's real responded accordingly.

> *"...the brightest version of you is on the other side of your fear."*

As you get to the next level of yourself, as you peel back the layers of self, the process can be excruciating. A chick doesn't hatch easily—it must eat away at its shell. Similarly, a caterpillar must break down before it breaks through the chrysalis. So too, the brightest version of you is on the other side of your fear. Take challenges head on, not as a way to solve them, but as an undoing of old ways of seeing, hearing, thinking, feeling, smelling, and living. With every challenge, you are humbled by your fear, so that your strength and courage must grow.

When I emerged on the other side of my immobilization, I clarified the story I want to tell with my life. Simply, I chose contribution, beauty, love and growth. I'm still learning what each of those values means in practice. As a glow-getter, life is constantly in transition and transformation. You go from one hurdle of meaning to the next. If you want all these big, juicy dreams, get ready to meet the next challenge. Get ready to define, refine, and choose power in every thought. Get ready for the highest and deepest version of yourself. To this day, ten years after my return, I choose the interpretation of that breakdown as a "breakthrough," dying to my prior, unaware self and a rebirth to an empowered, brighter self.

The stories that shape you are more than memories. They are what lives—and relives—inside your body, in every cell and heartbeat. Your soul is imprinted with the minuscule details of these ongoing moments that change your life forever. What I hope for you is not a complete destruction of your stories, but an understanding of what details and interpretations allow you to flourish.

With The Glow Effect process, you can create a personal culture that serves the genius that you are. The internal argument with reality disappears, and what remains is love: love for yourself, for others, and for whatever you encounter on your life path. When you haven't investigated your thoughts, feelings, and desires, you'll attach the same disempowering stories to any life circumstances. An authentic, genius you is in there, probably emerging more than you know. By coming back to such truth, you will glow and affect your world. Thus, two questions must be answered to guide you to the genius, glowing you: (1) what is your genius, glowing zone? And (2) how do you use your seeming disadvantages to move towards it?

DEFINING THE INDEFINABLE: YOUR GENIUS, YOUR PURPOSE, YOUR GLOW

As much as we want to think that our intellect drives us, our emotions, the sensations that we link to our thoughts, are what truly drives us. So, if you don't consciously plan how you want to feel, raise your standards, change your limiting beliefs, and change your strategy to get there, society, media, community, and family can hijack your life. Ok, that may be a bit harsh, but by not consciously choosing your own interpretation of events, you allow the world to choose for you.

Advertisers, for instance, are experts in cultivating sensational experiences with colors, imagery, and music. Celebrities receive millions of dollars for ads because of the emotional experiences they can convey. When you're in intense emotional states, anything unique that occurs consistently will become neurologically linked. When those unique things happen in the future, the same emotional experience is triggered. That is, you build beliefs and interpretations through repetitive emotional responses. This isn't necessarily a commentary on individualism, capitalism or advertisement. This is about transforming your emotional experience for self and world empowerment.

Empowerment through the genius zone does not mean you become an emotionless machine. Your "energy in motion" is mastered and pointed toward creation. Empowerment is an emotional release when you allow emotions to run through you, without attaching and wallowing in suffering. Let's be clear, every human experiences emotions. Fact. What's at issue is how you process them. Ultimately, all I've ever asked was what differentiates the processes of successful, vibrant, genius people in the world? What creates a glow-getter, a trailblazer, and a contributor to society? It relies on what I call, "glowing," as in the spherical light that allows you to bounce back, adapt to your environment, and learn from the world even while you stay at home. When dealing with feelings, interpretation, or decisions, the choice of a glow-getter is the one that brings you closer to genius. When you choose what to feel, you are no longer a victim of circumstances, you are an empowered glow-getter.

One thing is clear: human beings are not random—everything and everyone has reason for their actions, even if it's unconscious. Tony Robbins articulates,

> There is a single driving force behind all human behavior. This force impacts every facet of our lives, from our relationships and finances to our bodies and brains. Everything you and I do, we do either out of our need to avoid pain or our desire to gain pleasure.

Whenever anything happens in your life, your brain asks two questions: 1) Does this mean pain or pleasure? 2) What must I do now to avoid pain and/or gain pleasure? Your answers are what create a belief. I believe going to the dentist is painful, for example, but getting my teeth cleaned will bring me pleasure. Therefore, despite the pain, I get myself there. If you're struggling to accomplish something, consider how the short-term pain associations are outweighing the long-term pleasure.

Stories, the compilations of your beliefs, are the guiding force that tell you what will lead to pain and what will lead to pleasure. When you feel frustrated or overwhelmed, unable to make a change, it's because you're trying to change the effect, the emotions, instead of trying to change the cause, your pain/pleasure associations and the unwieldy stories that result. This is the most important lesson you learn in life: what creates pain for you and what creates pleasure.

Throughout your life, you learn to seek certain emotions as moving you toward pleasure. With culture and experience you develop unique, coding systems for what feels good and bad. This is your value system—the values that define glowing. Your glow relies on how you ultimately want to feel. What does your genius actually feel, look, smell, and taste like? You're shooting for the sweetheart, the cash, and the accessories, *and then* you'll feel joy, fulfillment, and success. What if, first, you get clear on the person you want to be (generous, loving, joyful, successful, and so on), *then* you design the wish lists? When you're clear on how you want to feel, your decision-making gets to the heart of your genius.

Your value systems shape your decisions and ultimately the direction of your life. If you're not clear about what is most important to you—what you stand for—you cannot create a basis for self-esteem, let alone make effective decisions. You link this indefinable, glowing state to values, to states of pleasure you want to move toward—love, learning, joy, success— and the states of pain you're trying to avoid—anger, resentment, jealousy, and sadness.

There are two types of values: the ends and the means. If glow is an end value, meaning living your genius, experiencing lots of love, and being the highest version of yourself, growth would be the means. So too, if love is your end value, perhaps family and money to care for your family are the means to reach that goal.

Paradoxically, the brighter you get and the more you want for yourself and the world, the more challenges you will face. Again, you have two choices in how to interpret these challenges: opportunities for growth or signs of destruction. Glow-getters choose not to become a victim of their circumstances. We choose to be a victor by using dismal circumstances, despite the short-term pain, as fuel for change and create the long-term pleasure.

What keeps you from making life changes: starting that diet, quitting the job you hate, or asking someone out on a date? All of these things could clearly bring you towards your genius, so why do you fail to act? You could lose the security of your job; you could start that diet and gain the weight back; or the babe could reject you—all painful. On the other hand, you could choose courage and find the height of your career, lose all the weight, or experience the most enlightening relationship of your life. You could cross the next threshold to your genius. The answer: you associate more pain to the short-term shift than the pleasure of the long-term gain. Your values aren't clear. Is the pain of waking up at 5:00 A.M and whipping your ass at the gym vital for the person you want to be? Does the pain of cutting your expenses and uncertainty of future income keep you from creating that career of your dreams? When you shift your associations of pleasure and pain, you move towards what's possible. That decision to remove self-inflicted pain and establish long-term pleasure—the pleasure of growth and strength—that's the force that makes you glow.

Indeed, sometimes you don't know what means will move you towards genius, which easily explains why you don't take that path. Yet, more often, you're shown what is healthy, life affirming, and fulfills your potential. There is no lack of empowering information. How many times have you said, "I know it's good for me to hit the gym, but that extra hour of sleep is too delicious;" "I'd like to skip the snack food, but a few chips won't hurt;" "Meditation is the key to transformation but I can't seem to get myself to sit still;" and "Those 20 self-help books I've taken apart on my shelf, I can't seem to implement anything." Why can't you be kind to yourself and create a life that radiates? Why is it that you can feel a tremendous amount of frustration, but still not change?

You haven't experienced *enough* pain.

We've all been in those jobs, at those weight levels, or in those relationships, where we say, "Enough is enough. Something must change." This is that transformational shift where pain becomes your ally. You've hit an edge of growth. Pain becomes a call to action. The action is to continue—to breakthrough instead of breakdown and give up. Like the chick cracking through the shell and the butterfly breaking out of the chrysalis, you have the opportunity to break through your limiting beliefs and experience genius.

Glowing genius neither happens overnight, nor is it an endpoint. Most people would rather hold on to what they have rather than take risks and journey toward what's possible. In order to glow, you must have a long-term focus. Most of the challenges you have in your life, like an indulgence in drinking, smoking, overeating, stress, or giving up on goals, come from the pain of short-term discipline. Take losing weight: early morning wake-ups to get to the gym, cutting out the delicious unhealthy foods, the burn of muscle change; because these are painful in the short-term, you must be motivated by the values of health, self-love, and accomplishment—the long-term pleasure of glowing genius. In this way, you can change anything by changing your belief associations.

Small decisions along the way can keep you a victim of a story that doesn't get you to the glow zone. It's the failure to persist, follow-up, manage your mental and emotional reactions, and to control what you focus on that keeps you mired in painful circumstances.

This brings us to the second question: if you know your values (a.k.a. what brings you into your glow zone), how do you meet them consistently?

THE SECRET TO CHOOSING MOMENT-TO-MOMENT GLOW

Glowing genius is a creative tension. As you delve into your values and create empowering stories, take on these perceived flaws and contradictions that make you gloriously multidimensional. If you want a bold, extraordinary life then you have to bring your full self into the game—cosmic love and worldly ambition, spirit and diñero, high standards and compassion. If you're showing up for life, then you won't be able to tell the difference between selflessness and self-serving, because it feels so good to give... or receive? Fulfillment, glowing genius, is the result of bringing your authenticity, disadvantages and all, to the table. Glow comes from embracing the highs of pains and lows of pleasure... or is it the opposite? Not just the politically correct and the well-behaved bits, not just your degrees and certifications, not just your passion, cause you need to flex some mental muscle. If you try to keep your most sacred ambitions off your weekly calendar, your most genuine traits off of your resume, and your beautiful vulnerability out of your relationships, then you're missing out on the power of real integrity.

This is the secret to choosing glow in every moment: allowing your dynamic nuances to show. Empowering authenticity allows you to keep promises that you make to yourself. When you're living in alignment with your values and your word, paying attention to when choices are out of line with your genius, you have integrity.

The source of workability, flow, power, and freedom in your life is integrity: keeping your promises and agreements. When you're aligned with your word, just like when a bicycle wheel is intact, your life works. If you mess up a spoke, it's not that the bike falls apart, peddling is just way more effort. Notably, integrity is not morality. We like to collapse it into moral uprightness—making "good" choices, doing the "right thing." Rather, integrity simply means whole, undivided, is or is not, sans the right and wrong.

"An integral being," Lao-tzu says, *"knows without going, sees without looking, and accomplishes without doing."* How you move through the world relies on integrating your word and your actions. Your self-esteem and confidence rely on this wholeness. When something feels off, you're misaligned with your promises and agreements. You feel separate and disconnected from yourself, which manifests in listlessness, malaise, and dis-ease. Traditionally we view disease as a degenerative process. Disease, however, can be understood as dis-ease, meaning "without ease" in the human body. For example, when we suffer from a pinched nerve or nutritional deficiencies, the mind and the body are in dis-ease. Health is not merely the absence of disease; health is when every part of the body is working together, effortlessly, relaxed and at ease.

While Part One was about connection to others, this shift into integrity creates a deeper connection with your soul, dissolving the tension in your body and mind. If your intuition has told you for a while that a job or boyfriend isn't the right direction, and you're doing, saying, or thinking things in conflict with your value system, your self-esteem will drop in proportion to that misalignment. You're out of integrity, and your glow will respond accordingly. Bottom line: until you start keeping promises to yourself, you'll feel off.

You have somewhere between 15,000-50,000 thoughts per day. You don't actually attach to people or things—you attach to these uninvestigated thoughts that you believe to be true in the moment. Thoughts are harmless in and of themselves. They're images rolling through your mind like a scroll of film. When you believe your thoughts without investigating them, you attach. Attaching to a thought means believing that it's true without inquiring. A belief is a thought about pleasure and pain that you've attached to, often for years. From the belief, you then generalize to identify patterns. For instance, you generalize that when you give your money to a bank, they'll give it back to you. Then you look for references or evidence to support this generalization. If you didn't have a sense of certainty, you wouldn't leave the house or trust anyone.

Your brain is specifically wired with a mechanism called a "Reticular Activating System (RAS)." The actual process of the RAS is complex, but the concept is simple. Your brain delineates the millions of stimuli that are thrown at you in every moment. Right now, regardless of where you are, there are millions of things you could focus on. Instead of darting around to all of the sounds, smells, colors, or thoughts, you're focusing on the letters in front of you. In your day-to-day decision-making, what you choose to focus on can make all the difference. If you have the thought, for example, that you won't make money as an actor, you may start to notice all the actors not making money as references to bolster that belief. Notably, evidence to the contrary is also present, but your RAS focuses on the supporting evidence for the thought you've set in place. Imagine how these references would influence your levels of fear and subsequently influence you reaching your genius zone.

The left cerebral hemisphere of the human brain is prone to fabricating these verbal narratives that are inherently not true. Director of the SAGE Center for the Study of Mind at the University of California, Santa Barbara, Michael Gazzaniga, describes,

> *The left brain weaves its story in order to convince itself and you that it is in full control... What is so adaptive about having what amounts to a spin-doctor in the left brain? The interpreter is really trying to keep our personal story together. To do that, we have to learn to lie to ourselves.*

The brain begins with a thought like, "I'm not smart," "All guys cheat," or "Only rich people are happy." The ego, with all its fear of obliteration, creates a rule to protect you from these frightening ideas. Rules could be about the past ("I didn't get the job because I'm not smart enough"), the present ("I don't have a boyfriend because all guys cheat"), or the future ("Once I start making money, then I'll be happier"). Eventually, beliefs become rules that orient your life. Every time you use terms or ideas with "should," "could," or "would," you're signaling a discord with reality. If you describe things how they should be (e.g. "He shouldn't have laughed at that"), what they could be (e.g. "If my boss yells at my work then he doesn't like me"), or why they are (e.g. "She failed math, so obviously she will never be successful"), you're projecting your thoughts onto what is true.

Can you see how a thought such as, "He shouldn't have laughed at that," conflicts with reality? He did laugh at that, so projecting your thought of what shouldn't have occurred only creates a tension in you. Or, what if your theory about your boss is wrong, and you spend years thinking he hates you because he yells? Your boss could have yelled at you because he stubbed his toe.

As Gazzaniga points out, in order to assure protection of our rules, we refuse to see any evidence to the contrary. When you believe your thoughts instead of what is true, you experience an emotional distress that we call, "suffering." Suffering includes a spectrum of effects from great sobbing and dramatics to a simple tension in the shoulders. While pain and difficulty are inevitable, this suffering in your reaction is optional.

Try this: close your eyes. Think of the things that you don't have: a mansion in Ibiza, a yacht in the West Indies, a billion dollars, maybe a job. Feel that sensation of lack, the feeling of being incomplete. This sensation is suffering, a natural alarm, warning you that you're attaching to these scarcity and toxic thoughts. When you listen and inquire into the thoughts, you can see that this suffering is optional. Take a deep breath and let the toxic thoughts go. They're just thoughts, not reality.

> *"In order to glow, your rules must lead you to empowerment. Only you can create the shift."*

Now imagine all of the things you do have: a roof over your head, food in the fridge, perhaps someone that loves you. Feel that sensation of having, of wholeness and abundance. This is where your genius lives. This is not about figuring out what's true—whether you are or are not abundant. This is about noticing how your thoughts and rules can disempower your body, mind, and decision-making. If you believe that you have to be someone else (prettier, stronger, a lawyer, a great golfer) to be successful or that someone else must change his or her business for your joy, you've become a victim, and your actions will respond accordingly. There is another way. You have a choice.

In order to glow, your rules must lead you to empowerment. Only you can create the shift.

Please understand that you don't create these thoughts because you're stupid or wrong. You unconsciously confuse rules with truth. In order to glow, you must know how to realize the power, your power, underneath the stories and rules. It's not the conditions or the events of your life that determine whether you glow, but attaching to thoughts, the beliefs that you connect to the events, that shapes your life.

The challenge is threefold: 1) you do not consciously decide what you're going to believe, 2) you misinterpret past events, and 3) once you adopt a belief, you forget that it's just an interpretation. And these beliefs have the power to create or to destroy your vision.

Misinterpretation occurs with small and big things. On the big scale, as in the South African, reconciliation exercise, I harbored the belief that my pain was insignificant because it wasn't as tragic as others' pain. This led to devaluing myself. On a much smaller scale, I created a story around my hair. At some point, I created the rule that I couldn't cut my hair above shoulder length, otherwise I would be ugly. After I got lice in fourth grade, a hairdresser butchered my hair into short layers. I cried like someone had torn off an appendage. Instead of seeing the beauty in myself, I held on to the story that without my long hair, I was no longer me. Yes, this is a silly story of a 10-year-old, but it has stayed with me for over fifteen years. I still struggle to get my hair cut. Perhaps this story doesn't hinder me on a day-to-day basis, but if for some reason I lose my hair or *have* to cut it, an empowered rule would change the quality of my life. The point is that when you bind yourself with certain rules, you're limited in what is possible. I challenge you to see how thoughts are inhibiting your growth. By grasping at these thoughts, forgetting that they're just thoughts, instead of seeing or pushing the boundaries, you stop unpeeling the layers towards your glow.

If you go by others' stories of how the world works or misinformed rules—"Money is the only factor of success," "Guys must pay the bill," or "Pill-popping is okay in moderation"—and they don't resonate with what is authentic to your empowerment, you'll feel out of alignment. *"Believe nothing,"* says Buddha, *"No matter where you read it, or who said it, no matter if I have said it, unless it agrees with your own reason and your own common sense."* In order to transform your reactions for your genius, your decisions regarding beliefs—what things mean— must transform.

Though it would be lovely to unravel all of the stories of the past, as glow-getters, we must look forward. Do you interpret the world as a personal affront or a challenge moving you towards your highest potential? Unfortunately, most people never ask this because they're busy making excuses, i.e. the reason I haven't realized my genius is because of my parents, lack of money, and an early life trauma. I'm sorry that you experienced that. I'm not taking away the pain of those circumstances, but your future is determined by your interpretation of events and the decisions you make going forward.

When I became a family law attorney, my emotions became erratic. I felt exhausted constantly. I was hungry all of the time. At first, these body issues felt like distractions pulling me away from what was "important": spreadsheets, my to-do lists, memos and briefs. Then, I realized that these things were signs of something deeper. *Should I be crying every other day? I'm not exercising frequently, why am I so tired and hungry?* Something was off. Your body is a beautiful vessel (yes, always beautiful) that has infinite lessons to communicate. The Universe, God, Buddha, Muhammad, Krishna, the big bang, put you in this body for a reason. You're not meant to be in absolute control of your body. I've found that I don't want to be in control. My body is always trying to tell me something. After a while of signs, instead of seeking control, I started listening. I wasn't feeling good, healthy, or worthy. Yes, we all have tough days, but when I was consistently feeling off, I had a choice in how to interpret it: shame, as in *There is something wrong with me*, or a sign of going the wrong direction. The disempowering, shameful thoughts make it easy to lose hope. Seeing everything as a miraculous sign, in contrast, empowers us to choose our response—accept the situation or change something. Hindsight is always 20/20, so when I eventually quit my job, and saw the signals as movements towards meaning, love, and contribution, I no longer was crying at the drop of a hat, looking for food 24/7, and staying in every night out of exhaustion.

A client, Elsie, told a parallel story with her relationships. She had been with her ex for nine years, when he cheated. They had been together for so long, she almost let it go. Then she started to get rashes, get angry at random times, and her weight started rising. She kept trying to change these symptoms with frequent visits to the dermatologist, gym, and wine store. When we explored the person Elsie wanted to be—strong, vibrant, loving—she felt that she was living life in contrast to those values. She didn't feel strong when she allowed this person who had caused her so much pain to still be part of her life. She was in constant fear that he would cheat again, which made her feel lifeless and stifled. And while she wanted to give love with no strings, this person made her feel depleted. Note that this isn't a morality issue, i.e. "Elsie should leave because it's the *right* thing to do." Rather, with Elsie's values, her way of being under these circumstances, misaligned with whom she wanted to be. She was out of integrity. Restoring her integrity allowed her to determine her course of action and her decision to break-up with him shifted everything. Despite the short-term pain involved with the break up, her skin cleared, she lost weight, and she had a long-term smile on her face.

You can't simply solve your problems by gathering new information or replacing one set of information with another—you must dissolve your old belief systems, shine light on the false foundations that hold these old belief systems in place, and actively and constantly build new ones.

Pop quiz! (Please don't let this evoke stories from childhood quizzes. This one will be easy. Promise.) Which meaning do you choose?

1. My ex broke up with me because... (a) I'm flawed or (b) I'm working on some challenges that I must resolve before I have a solid relationship.

2. I'm in debt because... (a) I'm bad with money or (b) I invested in things that I added to my life and I'm learning to make better investment decisions.

3. I've gained weight because... (a) I'm over-indulgent and lazy or (b) I fully enjoyed recent moments and plan to be more nourishing and loving to my body moving forward.

If you chose (a) for any of the above, you're not wrong. I repeat: integrity does not mean morality. You're simply out of alignment with growth. The choice of a glow-getter is movement towards the most glowing, and powerful version of you. Growing and glowing is who you are. Mistakes aren't mistakes at all, they're lessons revealing your genius. Instead of the shameful, I-am-not-enough interpretations, start with: "I am glowing—this is my natural state. Every difficulty is an opportunity to expose a dark pattern."

> *"The choice of a glow-getter is movement towards the most glowing, and powerful version of you."*

In sum, this is how we form our stories...

1. At some age (likely early), something happens. You make judgments about the incident—whether it provides you pleasure or pain.

2. The judgment creates subsequent feelings and thoughts: are these valuable experiences to repeat? Your judgment creates either a value to pursue or a pain to avoid.

3. Feelings and thoughts accumulate to form rules, i.e. happiness is important to me, and I'm only happy in a relationship; lawyers aren't trustworthy, and trust is the most valuable thing; I'm stupid because I wasn't in AP Math, and intelligence is paramount.

4. You acquire evidence or references to support such conclusions.

5. You construct a story around the rule, supported by evidence you've gathered.

6. The story permeates your being and forms your identity.

In order to dissolve the stories, ground yourself in the reality of every situation. Two elements for this:

1. Distinguish what happened from the meaning you've attached.

2. Consciously choose the meaning you want to create. Empower yourself.

Re-creating empowering stories cannot happen in a vacuum. They occur through relationships. In that way, every relationship can show you where your glow has dimmed and where you shine...

Four

Glowing Relationships:
A Power Practice

Your stories, your comprehensive interpretations of phenomena, are your direct connection to the world. While habits brighten or dim your glow, how you relate to the world's behavior determines how you create transformation. Your life is comprised of relationships: your relationship to yourself, your relationship to others, and your relationship to the material world (like money). No relationship or interaction is frivolous. Every contact is meant to foster your growth. In order to glow, (need I say it?) growth is mandatory. Relationships are those containers through which most is learned about life and ourselves. In an ordinary day, you encounter countless contrasting beliefs. Without consciously appreciating differences and engaging in an inquiry process, you project your own belief systems. Then you get uncomfortable and experience pain and fear when people surprise you. If you don't look deeply at who you are and your role in every interaction, through your uninvestigated thoughts and actions, you risk detriment to others. After doing intense internal work on your values, rules, and stories, the true challenge comes when you must maintain your integrity while relating to the world.

The right diagonal orbit of your glow-sphere is this interplay between the interpretations through which you relate to the world and the world's reflections of what you need for further inquiry.

Case in point: I had the opportunity to listen to two men from the streets of Detroit discuss women. My first impression of this was disgust and discomfort, so I walked away. Later on, I sat down with one of the guys and discussed the misogyny pervasive in his words.

"The way you talked about sleeping with multiple women was awful," I persisted.

"I don't disagree," he said, *"but do you think that name calling or judgment of our language then cutting off communication creates progress? What if you asked where those associations come from?"* I froze. He continued, *"My dad passed me and my mom on the street when I was eight and didn't say 'Hi.' My uncle owned a strip club. Let's begin by looking at how my beliefs and language came to be and go from there."*

Choosing the path of a glow-getter—associating pleasure with growth and learning—means that I must stand by my ideals of inquiry, not approach the world proselytizing or hoping everyone holds my beliefs. Please don't think that I'll ever condone misogyny. Through an interaction like this, I realized that I must look discomfort in the face, instead of walking away. I must choose to break down the barriers that separate us, perhaps inspiring an alternative view of women. I must take a stand for what I believe in and create a dialogue.

Thus, relationships with the world don't begin with changing others—they begin with...

THE RELATIONSHIP WITH YOURSELF: AUTHENTICITY

By taking responsibility for your own joy, you affect your world. All reflection, all that you do in this life, your ultimate purpose is simple: it is to be yourself, to bring your whole self to the table. By tapping into your authenticity, you access your glow. With enthusiasm as your guide, you can channel the gifts that make you come alive, and then in the awakening process, you attract people, places, and things meant to support your purpose. There is a give and take: by glowing, your aliveness enlivens the world.

I have many clients that come to me with relationship issues: both romantic and non-romantic. Frustrated, often sad, and angry, they seek to remedy the pain. My first point of entry is the relationship with the self. How often do we hear that you cannot love another until you love yourself? Here is the secret: your "flaws," your insecurities, and your avoided feelings are actually your assets. The qualities that make you feel weird—your sensitivity, body hair, or obsession with Hello Kitty— are what make you human and interesting. These qualities are what allow you to relate. In the process of loving these qualities, you access compassion for yourself and others.

When I went through a traumatic break-up, I realized that every relationship was doomed to fail if my relationship with myself wasn't developed. At twenty-five, I began the only relationship that will last the course of my lifetime. I courted myself. I took myself on dates, bought myself flowers, and wrote myself love notes. I learned my vulnerable qualities, and gave myself permission to be fully authentic in every opportunity, until I was able to say to myself, *I love you.*

Once your inner relationship is healed, relationships with the outer world will transform. Problems remedy themselves. In other words, The Glow Effect is the effect of your self-love. *"Love knows how to form itself,"* says Marianne Williamson, *"God will do his work if we do ours. Our job is to prepare ourselves for love. When we do, love finds us every time."* Self-loving occurs in three parts: your feelings, your body, and your interests.

1. Value Your Feelings: Calls to Action

At some point someone spread the rule that emotions are to be controlled and that they're just reactions to the events in our lives. We tend to avoid emotions as if they're a plague sent to attack when we're fearful and vulnerable. In some cultures (I'm thinking the professional realms), emotions are to be hidden, as if they're inferior to the intellect. Western society urges prioritizing the musings of the mind over the feelings of the body. Indeed, thinking is incredibly useful to survive in society. Yet, when a feeling comes up like fear, stress, hurt, or loneliness, we're prone to over-eating, over-drugging, and over-exercising. Instead of feeling, we turn to numbing. In an effort to avoid, suppress, and deny feelings, we destroy connection: both connection to others and ourselves. We're left at the mercy of emotions without a real mastery of how to use them for growth.

There is another way, a way that allows you to feel empowered. With every feeling, you have a choice: to feel or not to feel. Choosing to feel requires a "why?" —as in, "Why bother feeling the yucky feelings?" If feelings were just meant as annoyances, then you certainly have my permission to ignore them. Except they're actually meant as your intuition's signals, calls to action, that something is off. The effort to resolve the feelings in the mind or at the bottom of a bottle is fruitless. Feelings will stay until they're lovingly acknowledged and worked through. Poet Robert Frost answers, *"The best way out is always through."* We try to go around the feelings by avoidance, escape, and resistance. Frost distills the idea that if you really want "out," avoidance, escape, and resistance won't work—at least not long term. You must move "through" by feeling.

Feelings, especially the difficult ones, are not meant to be a hindrance to your glow. They're meant to point you in the direction of light. *"Depression was,"* Parker Palmer, renowned author, educator, and activist explains, *"...the hand of a friend trying to press me down to the ground on which it was safe to stand—the ground of my own truth, my own nature with its complex mix of limits and gifts, liabilities and assets, darkness and light."* Depression, clearly not a fun experience, is not the universe being hostile. It's the hand of a friend. We tend to be so disconnected from our bodies that we think the mind and resistance can get us out of the discomfort. Glowing asks you to dissolve the mind/body dichotomy, to go inward, to see that feelings cannot be resolved by the mind. In fact, when you avoid, escape, or resist, you're likely missing a very important sign that your body is trying to show you. Your intuition does not function in words. It requires you to feel. By feeling, you can value your feelings, instead of becoming a victim of depression, addiction, and destruction.

Easier said than done, right? Not necessarily. Begin by knowing that you have an inner guidance system. Notice times in your life when you feel at peace, when something feels wrong, when foods make you feel good. In others words, just feel. We have a tendency to run from too much sensation, so if you struggle with this, start small. Feel the clothes you're wearing. Feel the air on your skin. Then notice the bigger feelings come up. Stress, for example, has the ability to make you work harder and escape. What if you just took a moment (just a moment) to be with it? For the expert thinkers out there, I broke it into steps:

1. A feeling arises.
2. Pause and notice it.
3. Welcome it. Actually say to yourself, "I allow this feeling to come up."
4. Watch the feeling and breathe into it.
5. Notice the story that you create around it, e.g. what meaning do you attach to the feeling?
6. Acknowledge that the story isn't real. Imagine the sensations dissolving with breath.
7. Sit and watch the feeling as long as you can.

Acknowledge that by valuing your feelings, you're completely capable of handling what life gives you. Feeling is simply breathing and welcoming the body's reactions. Suffering and long-term discomfort occur when you *resist* the feelings.

One of the fundamental principles of a glowing life is high standards. When you raise your standards for yourself and your life, you will stretch yourself to meet them. You must get out of your comfort zone in order to live big. While these high standards are highly motivating and inspiring, the uncertainty is also high. If not felt and lovingly acknowledged, it can be extremely destructive. When you feel rejected or defeated, the result of expecting more than you receive is challenging. So do you lower your standards? Hell no. Keep those standards HIGH! You deserve an epic life. If this one person or thing doesn't fit, move on. Oh, but the disappointment stings... Still, do not let the emotion crush you.

I repeat: DO NOT LET THE EMOTION CRUSH YOU.

Instead of perceiving disappointment as a dream crusher, try seeing every emotion as an action signal. The message is not to stop your dreaming; the message is to adjust your expectations of this element. Take action to set and achieve a new goal immediately. Figure out something you can learn from this situation that could help you achieve the very thing you were originally after. Also, realize that you may be judging the situation too soon. Simply because the thing you want isn't happening now, doesn't mean you're being denied your dream. A delay is not a denial.

Perhaps the thing that you're disappointed about is only a temporary challenge. How many times have you wrapped your emotions around a new beau, job, or perfect golf shot, only to realize later that there was something to learn before you "scored"? If you always get what you want when you want it, you miss out on exceptional lessons that may protect you from disappointment in other ways or redirect you to something better.

Rejection is protection, and protection is re-direction.

Most importantly, realize that you and your life are not over. Reevaluate what you want, and develop an even more effective plan of achieving it, i.e. it may be time to refine your golf game or your mental game. Bottom line: cultivate an empowered possibility for what will happen in the future, regardless of what happened in the past. You choose the meaning of every feeling: does it crush you, or is it a call to action? How you value your feelings creates an emotional fitness, preparing your reaction muscles to endure greater feats. You grow stronger not by resisting and avoiding. You grow stronger by feeling and letting go.

2. Value Your Body: Stop Comparing and Find Your Power

In order to cultivate glowing energy, if you want to be sexy, radiant, and awesome, you must see that you already have those qualities in you. Remember, it is not the conditions of your life that determine whether you glow, but the MEANING that you create and attach to conditions.

You have power to change the meaning you associate with your body. Like we discussed, the challenge is that 1) you do not consciously decide what you're going to believe, 2) you misinterpret past events, and 3) once you adopt a belief, you forget that it's just an interpretation. How would your energy transform if you believed that your body is a vessel meant for achieving your genius? Our culture promotes the belief that any perceived physical flaws or difficulties means you're worth less. As a result, we try to gain control of our perceived inadequacies through self-hating tactics. Self-hate manifests in substance abuse, eating and exercise disorders, and physical manipulation. If you believe that you have to be someone else (e.g. prettier, stronger, thinner) to be sexy, you've limited the genius you already are. What if your flaws are your assets? Your quirkiness, boy-ish hips, and curly hair are your means to glow. Everyone has a different meaning associated with every feature: Straight hair is ugly, flat chests are preferable, heavy girls are sexier, shorter girls are cuter—but sometimes the opposite is true. "The grass is always greener" is a cliché for a reason. In other words, every feature could be a goldmine or curse, depending on the meaning you associate with it.

Revealing your glow, living life at your highest potential, challenges you to let go of the limiting beliefs that say what's possible. If the universe wanted you to be different, it would have created you differently. Instead, the universe gave you these assets for you to grow, learn, and realize that your glow has nothing to do with this external form. You must nurture your vessel so that you can be the most effective version of yourself and fulfill your personal mission.

By believing that your body is meant to teach you and expand your life instead of limit it, self-love will emerge. You'll set boundaries. No longer will you allow people to speak down to you or take advantage of you. You'll make health a priority—you'll get sleep, you'll exercise for strength instead of punishment, eat greens and good fats, floss and wear sunscreen. Your emotions will no longer need to be repressed— they'll be calls to action. More so, these insecurities are your access to connection. Experiencing the difficulty of a big nose or short legs cultivates your compassion for another's insecurities. You become accessible and loving.

In his book *Tribes*, Seth Godin describes the leadership that emerges from using what you have to cultivate community. He says, *"This is an opportunity for you—an opportunity to find or assemble a tribe and lead it. The question isn't, 'Is it possible for me to do that?'"* Now, the question is, *'Will I choose to do it?'"* You have the world at your fingertips when you cultivate self-love. You become the change you want to see, and people will gravitate toward that empowerment.

3. Value Your Desires: Live Life on Your Own Terms

If someone says, *"Come walk on my path, it's successful,"* you have a choice. You can think ill of their interpretation or say that it isn't your version of success. Hoping that your dear mom and dad will lay off isn't going to help you achieve your genius. All you can do is interpret the meaning differently. Rather than shame for your chosen path, you can hear that they love you with all of their heart and want you to experience what they see as successful. Your parents, co-workers, bosses, friends, lovers will press every button you have, over and over and over, until you come face to face with the parts of yourself and the desires that you don't want to see. The discomfort will point to your glow every time. You want others to cherish and respect your thoughts and feelings, but the bottom line is that you need to respect your own thoughts and feelings first.

I must acknowledge that when I attempt to get my dad to respect my path, I'm not respecting his path. Sure, we may have elements in common. We can agree that money for food is important, that it would be nice to have a roof over my head, and have some loving relationships in my life. Yet, it's my choice whether money equals $100 or $10,000, whether a roof means shingles or a tarp, and whether loving relationships mean gay, straight, one or many. Sooner or later, when you value your desires as worthy, you can see the "I-love-that-your-way-makes-you-happy-and-mine-makes-me-happy" version of relating.

It's up to you, and only you, to choose the experiences you want to create. Towards the end of writing this manuscript, I committed to a thirty-day writing challenge. For thirty days, including weekends, I woke up at 6:00 A.M. and wrote for three hours before I started my day. For most of the days when my alarm sounded, I felt like throwing my phone across the room. Yet, when I turned on the light and words began to flow, I experienced a deep feeling of accomplishment. Daily, I became an energetic match for success by keeping my phone intact and committing to my purpose. Like I said, this isn't about my version of success, you writing a book, or even waking up early. Glowing is about valuing your desires, identifying what experiences you want to create, and committing to create them.

Success, the accomplishment of a purpose, is not a thing—it's an experience. The accomplishment of purpose initiates a fantastic, high vibrational experience (think "happy (!)"). Like I mentioned, in order to get anything you want, including success, love, or a killer bod, you must create the experience before you get the thing that you want. In other words, because everything you want has a vibration, you must be the vibrational match of what you seek. Many people approach manifestation from a place of, "How can I get something to feel successful?" Instead, ask, *How can I feel successful and therefore be an energetic match for actual success?* First and foremost, value your desires enough to commit to cultivating a path to get there.

According to Tony Robbins, we are all driven to fulfill six human needs. These basic needs are not just desires or wants, but profound needs that serve as the basis of every choice. The six needs include:

> **Certainty:** The need for security, comfort and consistency.
> **Uncertainty:** The need for variety and challenges.
> **Significance:** The need to feel important, needed, wanted and worthy of love.
> **Love and Connection:** The need to feel connected and/or loved by other human beings.
> **Growth:** The need for development emotionally, intellectually and spiritually.
> **Contribution:** The need to give beyond ourselves.

The first four needs are the needs that we always find ways to meet, even if it is through violence, casting ourselves as the victim, or mental illness. For example, being depressed can meet the first four needs: you can be *certain* you'll feel sad tomorrow, you're likely *uncertain* whether you'll ever get the help you need, you feel *significant* because your sadness outweighs the hope of anything else, and you can *connect* with others over your suffering. Despite the contradictory elements, we need both comfort and variety, as well as individual importance and community. We all have these fundamental needs in order to move through the world. The last two needs are our personal development needs, which provide lasting fulfillment. Glowing comes from the optional needs: growth and contribution. How each of us meets these needs is so diverse that judgment is useless.

When I decided to do my thirty-day writing challenge, I committed to growth and contribution. My intuition screamed that I must write daily. Sometimes I complied, but more often, I didn't. When I didn't, I felt like my potential, my contribution to other glow-getters, was unfulfilled. The result was self-hate. My glow dimmed. By writing every day, I experienced growth: my skill and self-discovery evolved. Further, I felt feel like I was contributing to the world on a daily basis. My decision to write fulfilled my personal development needs so profoundly that my glow brightened. Again, this isn't about you committing to a writing challenge. Rather, this is about discovering what makes you light up and committing to the growth and contribution it takes to get there.

Seth Godin writes, *"It turns out that the people who like their jobs the most are also the ones who are doing the best work, making the greatest impact, and changing the most. Changing the way they see the world, sure, but also changing the world."* When you value your desires, the effect on your world will be extraordinary, and it will be on your own terms.

RELATIONSHIP WITH OTHERS: RELATIONSHIPS ARE CONTAINERS FOR GROWTH

> *"When you meet anyone, remember it is a holy encounter. As you see him, you will see yourself. As you treat him, you will treat yourself. As you think of him, you will think of yourself. Never forget this, for in him you will find yourself or lose yourself."*
> *-A Course in Miracles*

Your relationship with yourself and your unique gifts to the world are primary: they're your roots. Yet, roots do not grow for the sake of being roots. Roots deepen in order to grow a tree. Relationships are the tree. Trees are here to serve; they're homes and sources of life for many;

this is their purpose. Yet, without rooting and food, they wither and cannot give: they die. Their relationship to the earth becomes a beautiful symbiosis of give and take. The same is true of the human being. You live to give and serve. This is your purpose: to express your truth so authentically that you can support life. Like trees, you also need firm rooting and fuel so that you may give from abundance. Your relationship with others is this symbiosis. You cannot live in isolation, without purpose, but you also cannot be without this grounding source of life from inside. Bringing it back: our relationship to the world and others is the purpose and the source of life.

Got it. Relationships are important. Now what? You can do self-work until cows fly, but if you're not using the outside world to deepen your growth, your power is limited. If you want to glow and affect glow in others, you must dive deep. This is what relationships ask of you. They ask you to experience, communicate, and co-create with other beings experiencing a vastly different reality. If you virtually have the same background, even the same parents, every person in your life has a different reality. When you relate, your goal, at a minimum, is to find commonalities in each reality. This is communication. *What language can I use in order for us to meet the desired result?* Body language, Spanish, energy, laughter, tears are all forms of communication. Attempting to understand another person's use of many languages is where conflict, discomfort, and pain may arise. At the same time, you're able to learn and expand. Relationships become containers for growth. In every conversation and relation with another you have a choice: you can impose your reality or seek to understand another's reality. You can expose your dark corners or fight to keep them hidden.

Like we discussed earlier, your rules are deeply influenced by your cultural frameworks. Being part of two very contrasting communities for many years, the legal world and yoga world, inevitably created difficulty in my relationships. Some would judge me for not fitting into either world fully. I would judge others for not speaking my yoga/legal language. Comments like, *"Why would you ever start a blog?"* came from the legal realm, which contrasted with, *"Express your Truth—hold nothing back,"* coming from the new thought, spiritual realm. I decided to use my values of love and contribution to turn my relationships around. I saw that such comments could result in stagnating, hurtful interactions, or they could be containers for growth. I noted everyone's opinions and whether such comments were reflections of them or me. More often, they were speaking to their own insecurities.

It's like the practice of a growing, bilingual child. As a bilingual child grows up, she has to learn two languages. In the beginning, there is a major learning stagnation. She has to learn twice the amount of words and concepts as the monolingual child. Eventually, there is a major learning curve, and she begins to learn both with ease. Even more beautiful, she is able to use her knowledge of both languages to deepen her understanding of words and concepts. When you wear multiple hats throughout the day or even try to relate to others who don't speak *your* language, you too have to broaden your words and concepts. Similar to the bilingual child, it is easy to get stuck on the contrasting words or views. Here is the potential for the learning curve: interactions can be an opportunity for a deeper understanding of you. Ask: *Why is this person in your life? What can you learn about yourself from this interaction?* Begin to notice how you relate to others. These interactions are not meant to break you. They're meant to deepen your language skills. While the bilingual child builds bridges of understanding between people who can't understand each other, a glow-getter can help facilitate understanding between two people or cultures. We're ambassadors of change.

Of course, all of this learning and growth requires... yes, you guessed it—vulnerability! To expose your wounds to people you care about—the icky stuff, the ego stuff, the personal growth, and the dark corners that you haven't yet mastered—is a vulnerable experience. Letting others see your secret wounds and ungroomed parts can trigger core fears of rejection and abandonment, of withdrawal of love. Yet, to bear witness to someone's wounds is a privilege. It's an opportunity to deepen a relationship, beyond the idealistic views you might have, into the real truth of both your light and shadows.

When you are vulnerable enough to expose those corners and own them, and when you then ask those you love to be gentle and they choose to do so, it starts to feel like love. When your corners are illuminated, there's nothing you have to do to "fix" them. Corners do the most damage when you're blind to them and they can inadvertently poke around and hurt people without your awareness. You may leave shrapnel in the wake of poking, and once you realize this, you may feel even more motivated to hate your corners rather than treat them with loving compassion. Don't fret: once you see your corners, they automatically start to dissolve in the light. Like bugs that scurry away when the floodlights flip on, your dark corners, once seen, start healing themselves.

After all of this we know two things: (1) You act out the love model you learned from your parents on other people, and (2) A relationship is going to bring out the unexamined wounds. The key to transforming anything lies in your ability to reframe meaning.

"Enlightenment," meaning to provide with light, is our goal. It's the key to intimacy. In-to-me-see requires true authenticity. Moving through the dark corners that surround your glowing self, working through all issues causing you to attack, defend, need, control, grasp, and avoid—the layers of ego—in that place of illumined authenticity, then you are at your most intimate. How much more intimate can you be than the realization that we are connected already? You become more intimate with life itself, because you are truly stripped down. This is vulnerability: growth and contribution. At the realization of connection, you go beyond just attracting that intimacy; you sustain it through service once it gets there.

"Here's what happens in relationships between men and women (or any kind really)," Marianne Williamson explains, *"if each person is not aligned with god (or the sacred, if that makes more sense to you), then their childhoods and past relationships come into play and collide into one another. You get a collision of egos, with each person taking himself or herself to hell."*

If you're living from a place of insecurity and survival, where it feels like you're flailing to stay afloat, you will feel self-centered, out-of-balance, and unfulfilled. Loving from a lack of self-worth will deplete you more. Survival mode can feel like you're working hard and getting nowhere, like you've fallen into quicksand and you're struggling to get out. Most people live in fear that they'll either lose their job, the money they already have, their health, or their partner. The only true security in life comes from knowing that every single day you're expanding your character through connection to the world.

Many of us, particularly the female kind, are trained to think that this kind of exposure comes by putting others first. This is false. When you put others, family, friends, loved ones, before yourself, you sacrifice your growth. What you end up giving to your world is a depleted, broken you. How much more loving would it be to give from abundance?

"You're too important to melt into another."

Please note the discrepancy here. Giving from depletion is no longer from love: it is desperation. You love by revealing your glow first, by exposing our childhood wounds and past triggers, not poking at another's. True love comes from abundance when each party brings their exposed, vulnerable self to the table. This is the boundary principle: in order to be your fullest self, to glow, you must know what brings your sphere into balance. When someone, regardless of how important in your life, asks you (or doesn't have to ask you) to sacrifice what makes you whole, if you don't set boundaries, then you're no longer whole. This all-encompassing, head-over-heels, giving-all-you-have thing we see in the movies only means that you lose yourself.

You're too important to melt into another.

Frequently, you hear, "I'm attracted to the hard-to-get types." We have come to see hard-to-get as a negative character trait. Perhaps, your attraction to this is revealing what you need to cultivate in yourself. "Hard-to-get" is deep self-respect for worth with clearly defined boundaries. Unfortunately, setting boundaries has gotten a bad rap. We say it's selfish or define this type of woman as a "bitch." Just because you set clear boundaries doesn't mean you speak with anything other than loving kindness. Think of it this way, someone who defines her boundaries kindly is actually showing a deep self-love. Instead of her actions being selfish or bitchy, she is requesting a more loving reality for herself, which consequently creates a more loving world. This is a heroic practice, which takes ongoing, constant refinement. The more you set boundaries with people that you think should be your first priority, the more your worth will rise. *You* become your first priority.

YOUR RELATIONSHIP WITH THE WORLD: MATERIALS AND MONEY

Can you talk about consciousness, beliefs, and relationships without talking about moneymaking? How you make ends meet is a portal to personal and collective growth. Let's turn up the light on your material desires, because when you set your own light free, you become a veritable force of nature. For that is what a miracle is: a shift in thinking which then shifts your experience. This shift in perception, your willingness to look beyond the surface of materials, enables you to invoke a different set of possibilities moving forward. It enables you to look beyond what's happening to what *could* be happening, creating the space for something new. It places you on a new ground of being. It can do for you what you can't do for yourself.

Your internal abundance is ultimately the source of your external abundance. Who you *are*, not just the services you provide, creates money. A glow-getter doesn't want energy in the form of money to *get* things. A glow-getter seeks to exchange energy in order to *change* things. When the energy you're putting out is filled with the consciousness of love, then the energy flowing back to you comes in whatever form most serves your good. *"Energy,"* Einstein says, *"cannot be created or destroyed, it can only be changed from one form to another."* Making glow the bottom line doesn't mean that you must give everything away or that you'll never charge for your services. The principle of a glowing exchange gives energy to both the giver and the receiver.

Glowing means knowing you're on earth for a purpose and that the purpose itself will create opportunities for its accomplishment. The world reflects back to you how much you value yourself, which relies on your belief systems and values of such a purpose. A purpose, a calling, is being the person you're capable of being. It's an extension of who you are. Giving energy for this purpose requires receiving energy in return. Thus, instead of asking, "How do I make more money?" with a shift in money beliefs, ask first, *What's the money for?* This allows a shift from an economic ordering principle to a humanity ordering principle. It allows whatever we do to be a conduit for creating the most beautiful world. Since money is energy, accruing it can mean power. This doesn't mean being the captain of consumerism or taking care of just family or yourself. Accruing energy is about a conscious sense of responsibility. In the service of a common endeavor, you can create a glowing world.

This shift from consumption to purpose relies on transforming childhood programming. First, recognize you are not at the effect of mortal limitation. Your mother isn't your real mother, and your father isn't your real father. You are more than the mortal self. As a creation of the universe, in the image of a creator, you're entitled to the miracles to which every child of the universe is entitled. You are at the effect of the world you identify with—if you live in the world of scarcity, you meet limited circumstances with limited thoughts. For example, if your thoughts are "Money doesn't grow on trees," "There are no jobs," or "A business doesn't happen overnight," your circumstances will respond accordingly. Instead, approach the limited conditions with the law of divine recognition—the universe will compensate for any limit in the material world. In an abundant worldview, there is no lack—there is no recession. Think about how many Fortune 500 companies started during a recession. Thriving is possible at any time. The meaning with which you meet a circumstance is everything.

If you judge the creation of wealth, you will sabotage yourself. For glow-getters, our spiritual stories may create shame and embarrassment around *wanting* to make money. Generalizations about the rich being bad or poor people being good are B.S. (belief systems). Not every rich person made their money unethically, and not every poor person is lazy. No socioeconomic group has a monopoly on righteousness. The fact is that nothing beautiful happens when money stops circulating (Think: breadlines and food banks). A fluid exchange of energy is always necessary. Judging anything glowing and fabulous will block the flow of greatness into your life. Beware of the power of your unrecognized beliefs.

Again, rather than asking, "What do I do?" shift your perception of what money means by starting with a different story: *who do I be?*

What limiting beliefs or judgments are you willing to let go of?

_____

_____

_____

_____

_____

What's the new reality around money that you want to create?

_____

_____

_____

_____

Who do you need to be in order to step into that new reality?

_____

_____

_____

Anytime you see someone who has what you want, celebrate it, instead of judging it. There is only a scarcity of resources if that's what you focus on.

If you came from a family culture of financial fear and lack, you may pinch your pennies, be wary of investing, and regardless of how much money you save, still feel there will never be enough. At the other end of the spectrum, if you had a parent with a debt issue, you may find yourself spending beyond your means and then playing all sorts of "management" games to get the bills paid just in the knick of time. The stress and drama that comes from spending and trying to play the system becomes how you relate to money. The good news is, just like the architectural blueprint of a house, you can change your mind's framework. To move from the fear of financial lack into the freedom of financial abundance, clearly see your current blueprint:

o   What was your family culture about money?

o   Who controlled the finances?

o   Was money used as a reward?

o   Was money withheld as a punishment?

o   As a child, did you worry about money?

o   Were your basic needs met?

o   Did your parents fight about money?

o   What did your parents or caregivers teach you about money?

Take time to really dig deep and *feel* what the financial climate was growing up. Once you write down your answers, you will gain insight into your money beliefs.

The second step in creating a healthier relationship to money is to realize the view of abundance. Your parents taught you what they did and that became your reality about money, which means that none of it is inherently true or permanent. Many parents pass their money fears down to children thinking they are protecting or preparing them for the *way* it is. The way it was for your parents does not have to be the way it is for you. Family systems teaching children money-management skills, a strong work ethic, and concrete tools create a more abundant blueprint. Financial fear creates constriction around money. Since you are made up of energy, feelings of constriction block your flow of abundance and cloud your ability to see opportunities for financial gain.

Here are three tips for creating a new money blueprint:

1. Financial Literacy
With not just literacy, but *financial* literacy, you can go from working for money to having money work for you. What defines something to be an asset or a liability are not words, but numbers. When you understand what the numbers are telling you can understand accounting and cash management, and ultimately analyze investments. If you think that money is the problem, you have to change money. If you realize your financial literacy is the problem, then you can learn.

Instead of wanting anything outside of yourself to change when it comes to money, recognize it's way easier to change yourself.

2. A Vision Board

Create a visual collage of what you want in your life. I use a corkboard so I can change the pictures and words as life changes. This vision is not just for the things you want like the job, the car, and the house of your dreams, but also for the people you admire and the energy you aspire to emulate. Look at the board a few times a day, and engage all of your senses to create the full experience of actually having what is on the board and embodying the qualities of the person you envision.

3. Present Moment Awareness

The ability to be here now is an essential part of changing any inherited blueprint. The only way to change ingrained thought patterns is to be aware enough, in the present moment, to stop and change the thought. You can achieve this through breathing exercises, daily meditation, and mind-body connection. Once you become the observer of your thoughts, you can figure out which are fear-based and not serving your purpose and which are opportunities for you to create the life of your dreams. By creating the ability to be present in your life, you create the opening to catch the fear-based thought before it becomes your reality.

4. Mindful Speech

Be aware of the way you talk about money, and change the language that is not in line with your goals. You could say, "I can't afford it" or "How can I afford it?" One is a statement and one is a question. One lets you off the hook to be a victim around money, and the other forces you to think. You become powerful in the shift. Use positive words of abundance instead of negative words of scarcity. You create change with the words you use, the thoughts you hold, and the feelings they inspire.

Money and material consumption can be a taboo topic, especially if you came from a belief system without a money dialogue. I challenge you to get raw and honest about how you relate to your purpose and money. Glowing means knowing that the universe supports you in creating the good, the holy, and the beautiful in an abundant way. And it's in the third orbit that you can move into such potential...

"Glowing means knowing that the universe supports you in creating the good, the holy, and the beautiful in an abundant way."

How to Live to Your Potential and Affect the World

LEFT DIAGONAL ORBIT

What is Real and Your Potential

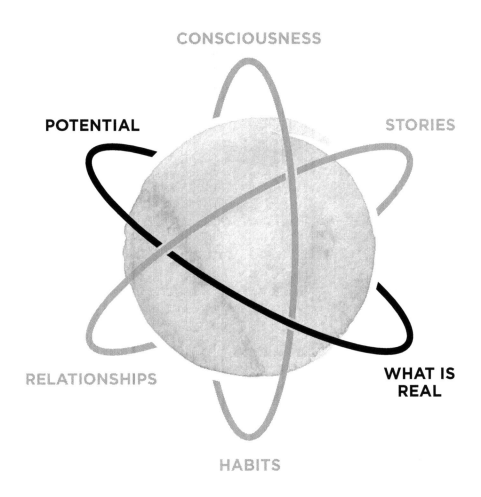

CONSCIOUSNESS

POTENTIAL

STORIES

RELATIONSHIPS

WHAT IS
REAL

HABITS

Shine A Little Light...

If you choose love and allow your stories to become empowered light beams, you'll begin venturing into your genius zone. Yet, you're not fully experiencing genius until you create an effect from your glow. You're not there until your energy touches, moves, and inspires others to create a transformation in their own world. So, what do you want to create? What will leave you so fulfilled that you're overflowing glow lights the world?

The journey of creating a tangible effect—starting a business, building a relationship, or becoming the glow you were always meant to be—is not linear. Part Three is this left diagonal orbit of your glow-sphere: the movement between presence, accepting, and loving what's real, to realizing your potential. In Part One, you expanded your consciousness (shifting into love instead of fear); in Part Two, you discovered how you relate to the world (creating empowering stories to define your success, joy, and glow); in Part Three, you'll explore the chaotic, glow-effect journey from presence to potential.

Part Three begs the question: once I glow, how do I affect results?

Just like every other orbit, to delineate between what is and potential is almost useless. In the glow journey, you'll constantly swing between the poles: acceptance and change, presence and ambition, certainty and uncertainty. No matter. Part of your glow effect is embodying your contradictions, which is exactly what must happen in order to love what is.

Personally, I can feel schizophrenic when I embody contradictions. One extra loud voice passionately screams, *GO LIVE YOUR DREAMS!* Another one mutters in judgment, *Don't be ridiculous. Work harder and pay the bills.* The Glow Effect is a delicate balance of surviving and thriving—how can you make the difficulties that life throws you your catalyst for transformation, while also making a living?

I've always paralleled this duality to my parents: my practical, introverted, conservative-minded father, named one of the "Best Dermatologists in Pittsburgh," versus my extroverted, spiritual, and inquisitive mother, deeply loved not only for what she does, but who she is. I'm proud to say that I'm well trained to live both frames of mind. Somewhere along the line, however, I was convinced that I had to choose to be like only one parent, i.e. I can't be·both ambitious and spiritually in-tune; I can't be a lawyer and a coach; I can't make money while living the beauty of my dreams. I have to choose one path and stick with it.

First, I went the full-on dreamer route: struggling actor, struggling activist, struggling yoga teacher—with the intention of love and joy. Yet, the struggles to pay bills, save money, and give when I didn't have enough for myself caused a glow burnout. Then, I tried the practical route: lawyerdom. My intention was to apply that struggling activist thing to this financially promising route, but I came up short. The money was nice, but it didn't feel like my own: too much of me was missing. Spirituality was nowhere in the equation, so many other values weren't met on a daily basis.

Here is what I didn't say about my parents: they're still happily married; there is no "versus." Their incredible, contradicting selves have complimented, pushed, and expanded one another for over thirty years. In other words, their contradictions are what make them powerful, trailblazing and influential. Passion and dreaming is the *fuel* and *destination* for practical fulfillment. Practicality and strategy is the *vehicle* to get from point A to point Z. If you're not fully living these trailblazing contradictions, waking up with passion and still able to pay the bills, then you're never going to get anywhere. It's time to clarify what magical voice in your head is muffled. We all have the capacity for both.

To live in an increasingly industrialized world means worldly ambition, but if you have any shred of discontent with a cold, industrial mind-set, spiritual practices can be appealing. This modern/spiritual tension doesn't mean havoc: the tension is what creates progress. Instead of trying to whittle away ambition or hippie tendencies, acknowledge that this tension is present for a reason. While unity is your source and connection to humanity, you are nothing without the tension of groundedness and possibility.

How does your oneness and connection step beyond itself and generate the many and the new? In other words, how can the sphere, a.k.a. you and your consciousness, create ideas, other beings, and transformations of yourself? Well, with a mirror, says Schneider, author of *A Beginner's Guide to Constructing the Universe*. By contemplating itself, reflecting its light, and casting its own shadow, the circle needs another circle to replicate. The line is drawn across the two centers of the circles. Oneness is the goal paramount; two-ness is what keeps things moving and creating.

We require two points, duality, to appreciate oneness. Alignment needs an opposite to even know that there is anything but unity. Opposites create a tension that occurs in all human experience as any relationship, contrast, or difference. It is the root of all birth and creation. Exactly two people of opposite gender, no more or less, produce a child. When cool, dry air penetrates warm, wet air, rain results. Two poles of a battery, positive and negative, are required to complete an electric circuit. You need darkness to appreciate your light. Duality shows how spirit consciousness is not only a path to oneness, but it is also the creator of reality. In the opposition, worldly ambition and spirituality tap into and produce a progressive and beautiful effect. That is, the ideas and innovations that the world needs rely on you being your authentic ambitious AND spiritual self.

We tend to think that duality is to be avoided. If we just work harder, meditate more, make more money, we could eradicate the darkness from our light, the rest from our awakening, the novice from our expertise. *"The paradox of the [polarity],"* Schneider explains, *"is that while it appears to separate from unity, it's opposite poles remember their source and attract each other in an attempt to merge and return to that state of unity."* In other words, we need polarities to be whole. We need rest to refresh and be effective. We need the beginner's mind for true growth. By embodying our contradictions, surviving and thriving, ambition and presence, and so on, we can accept the tension already present. The key is to change the way we interpret the tension.

As we discussed in Part Two, we have a myriad of choices in how we interpret circumstances. Think of *David and Goliath*, both the old age tale and Malcolm Gladwell's book. The giant, Goliath, appears at first glance to have the advantage. Contrary to first glance, David, quick and accurate with the slingshot, was the one with the advantage over Goliath. Gladwell argues that dyslexia or losing a parent, what seem like disadvantages, may be more advantageous than an Ivy League education or wealthy parents. Perhaps it's not wholly an advantage to experience trauma ("I want more pain in my life," said no one ever), yet the absence of it doesn't assure success. The fact is that these circumstances are reality. How you interpret them determines your future.

As a result of poorly defining advantages, Gladwell explains, *"We make mistakes. It means that we misread battles between underdogs and giants. It means how much freedom there can be in what looks like a disadvantage."* If you're stuck interpreting your past as a victim, i.e. "I haven't had this or that disadvantage, therefore I'm doomed," you miss the advantages of your pain. Your glow effect emerges from accepting reality as it is, then using these seeming disadvantages to create a bright path for others.

Before I inquired into my interpretations of circumstances, I took everything personally. Small thoughts could somersault into gigantic theories about why life is so terrible and how everyone thinks I'm crazy and weird. This resulted in feelings so discouraging and frightening that I struggled to get out of bed. When I did get out of bed, I had to force myself through life: *Study harder—you're not smart enough; workout more—you're not thin enough; give more—you're not kind enough.* An investigation into what is present breaks down toxic thoughts and reveals your natural genius. Inquiry reveals that what you think shouldn't be, should be. It should be, because it is what it is; no thinking will change that. It doesn't mean that you condone or approve of what is: it means that you can accept the situation without resistance.

Byron Katie, creator and prolific writer of this inquiry process, recommends four questions:

1. Is that true?
2. Can I absolutely know that this is true?
3. What happens (how do you react) when you believe that thought?
4. Who would you be without that thought?

Then turn the thought around, meaning if you think something "shouldn't be" then try it "should be"—ask which one is more accurate? What is real is generally the truer option. With each question you reveal an opening between the thought and what is. When you can see that thoughts are merely our projections onto reality, you can stop resisting what is true. Byron Katie explains,

> *I am a lover of what is, not because I'm a spiritual person, but because it hurts when I argue with reality. We can know that reality is good just as it is, because when we argue with it, we experience tension and frustration. We don't feel natural or balanced. When we stop opposing reality, action becomes simple, fluid, kind, and fearless.*

Reality is what is true: nothing more, nothing less. Where reality is concerned, there is no "what it should be." There is only the business of is-ness—only what is, just the way it is, right now.

You struggle to accept what's real since you've had uninvestigated stories snowballing your whole life. When you open up these stories, you begin to see how statements like, *"We shouldn't be in this financial crisis," "We're not working hard enough to eradicate violence," "There aren't enough good men out there,"* may not be true. I believed these statements at one point, too. They seem loving and well intentioned, but they created angst in my belly. *Is it really true that we shouldn't be in this financial crisis? Are we sure that we're not doing enough to prevent violence? Can I absolutely know in my gut that there are not enough good men?* When I dug for the answer, I saw the is-ness: the answer is that it is what it is: no more, no less. If you choose to focus on the lack of good men, you'll get what you put out there. None of the generalized projections of the way things *should* be can be true. Why? Simply because they're not. Stop should-ing all over yourself, otherwise you'll get mired in a disempowering illusion. It's not that a global or personal financial crisis should be ignored. You don't get lazy and give up because you're stuck with reality. I'm saying that only once you accept the reality as is, can you move forward into your potential.

The goal here is beyond putting the past in the past like we did in Part Two. The goal is to see that nothing has meaning without your projection. There is no inherent value in anything. Everything is empty and meaningless. Rather than seeing this as bleak, recognize that you've just created a clearing. Like when foliage parts in the forest, the sun beams into the space. The result is freedom, an opening for any possibilities to come to life. Thus, when we can accept the realities of the financial crisis, recognizing only the facts of budget deficits and lack of jobs as true (even though that term "crisis" presupposes a dismal interpretation), then we're able to shift perception about the possibilities for a solution.

Before we discuss how to effect a shift in perception, let's create the clearing.

Start by writing. Write down the thoughts, beliefs, and stories that cause you pain, anger, resentment, or sadness. Go wild! Complain and blame your parents, your neighbor, your partner, the Middle East. Address the people that have hurt you, the people that you're jealous of, the people that annoy you, the people that didn't give you the time of day, the people you've never met and haven't tried to meet. "My dad didn't pay attention to me." "My mother never accepted me." "Why can't the peace process happen in Israel and Palestine, dammit?!" "My coworker is always so negative." "I'll never have the body I want."

Notice the ongoing thread throughout your stories, the victimizing, this shouldn't happen, I shouldn't have to experience this, life is unfair. By thinking that someone should or shouldn't do something or something should or shouldn't have happened, you're mentally arguing with what is real. It doesn't empower you, and it doesn't change anyone. This is the opposite of the glow effect; the only effect of should-ing is discord.

Next, acknowledge what is real. Ask of your thoughts, *Can I know 100% that this is true?* The question brings up a sensation, an opening for acceptance of what is. So too, the answer reveals another sensation: the peace of release. Once you acknowledge what is real, the next step is to ask, *Whose business is this?* Whose business are you in when you're thinking that thought? There are three businesses: your business, others' business, and the universe's business (i.e. the weather and similar things you can't control). When you think that someone or something other than yourself needs to change, you're mentally out of your business.

Suppose your thought is that your friend should call you back. Ask, *Is this true? What do I think that would allow?* Your answer may be: *Yes, if she calls back, then I'll feel like I have my plans set for the day. I'll feel less chaotic.* You're saying that it is her business whether you feel chaotic or not. But, that's your business! Further, if she calls you back, will you really feel less chaotic? Do you absolutely know that's true? Another shoe could drop and chaos ensues. So ask again, do you really know that it's true? To think that you know what others should be doing is always to be out of your business. Even if the intention is love, it is pure arrogance, and the result is tension, anxiety, and fear.

If one of my friends said to me, *"You're not a great friend,"* I can honestly say, *"You know, my love, that makes sense. I'm always writing and coaching. I'm rarely there for you. Thank you for letting me know. How can we change this?"* My friends and family are incredible beings: they tell me what I may not see. I inquire into my thoughts, actions, and stories to see if they're right. So far, they're spot on. I could go outside myself, get defensive, and attack them, attempting to change their minds. In fact, one way to know something is true is when you get defensive. When I block it off and go to war with the person, mentally or physically, discomfort comes with it. Or, I can go deep inside and search for a truth that will light me up.

As a lover of glow, of truth, I want to know what that truth is—what is real. The best part? It works for good stuff too! When people say I've made a difference in their lives, I can go inside and find that. I don't have to go outside, profess my gratitude, and work to prove it. They're right. I'm right. My parents, boss, ex-boyfriend are all right—always. I either get to realize it or suffer. I am what they say I am, because it's real to them. Anything I feel that I need to defend against keeps me from realizing me, and bringing out what is true and unchanging.

Accepting what's real gives us a way to change the projector (the mind and the occurring world), instead of changing the projected (the words or action) or the projectee (the result: person, situation, thing) onto which you're projecting. It's like there is a piece of lint on the camera you're using to view the world. Rather than changing the images or getting a new camera, you're just removing the lint.

Let's not look at the potential of your being just yet: let's look at your being right now. Who is the essential glowing you? When you're clear, stripped down to your authentic reality, people effortlessly love you. Love is all that you're able to project or see. They have no choice. It is the ego with its fearful perceptions that tells you that you're in lack, empty or void of something, and you need things on the outside to make you feel safe, serene, love or wholeness. This is the biggest illusion ever. And it keeps you reaching outside of yourself to people and things to make you feel secure. This makes you a victim rather than an empowered creator of your own reality.

The whole world is your story, your projection, which is reflected back to you on the canvas of your projection. When the storyteller changes—the projector of the story—your projection of the world changes. If you want something to transform, then you have to know where you're beginning. You must face how the world is occurring to you, not with judgment or criticism, but with honesty and clarity. Remember in Part One when we discussed that "occurs" means a perspective of reality and Agassi's view of a tennis ball? His way of being in response to the tennis ball cannot be transformed without shifting his context of the ball. If you're experiencing fear and suffering, it's not the fear and suffering that need to shift. Those are real. It's your context of reality, how the situation is occurring to you, that is the source of the conflict.

It takes courage to look at what's working and not working. Workability means things are flowing. You put in a minimal amount of effort and things just jive. You feel freedom and power. No need for force. Imagine a bike wheel, or if you're a yogi, consider the body. Things work when they're in alignment, right? If you mess up a spoke or move a posture out of alignment, it's not that things fall apart, they're just way more effort. Again, another term for this is "integrity," meaning whole, undivided. Integrity is often collapsed into moral uprightness—making the "good" choices, doing the "right thing." Integrity is actually a phenomenon in and of itself. It has to do with authenticity—being true to you. It is the source of workability. When you do or say something that is out of alignment with something you believe or promised, it's like trying to lift a weight with your shoulder popped out of the socket or your bike wheel missing the rubber. It still works, but with major repercussions.

The trick is to learn how to objectively look at your life without judgment: to become a detached observer. It works or it doesn't. Period. A working life doesn't mean you're good and a struggling life doesn't mean there is something wrong with you. That collapses integrity and morality.

Before The Glow Effect process, when I got really honest, I saw that some areas of my life were beautifully easy, while other areas were a struggle. Instead of brushing the unworkable areas under the rug, I got clear on what wasn't working with this process:

First, separate the areas of your life. What's important to you? The areas I listed were:

> Career/TGE/Finances
> Family/Friends
> Health/Spirituality
> Romantic Relationships
> Relationship to making a difference in the world

Other options are Home Improvement, Hobbies, Self-Care, and so on. Things can be grouped however you see fit. If you'd like, you can have 20 categories.

Next, rate those areas on workability. On a scale from 0 to 10, with 0 being not working at all and 10 being perfect flow. I discovered that my areas of family and health were a 9, at least. Those areas just work for me. But before you go and think that I'm so lucky, I rated my business career and romantic relationships at a 5 and 3, respectively. We all have our stuff.

Third, consider that the areas that you rated lower are where you are out of integrity. In other words, ask yourself, *What promises and agreements were broken in those areas?* With this process, I saw that the two areas that weren't working, career and romantic relationships, were in conflict. I had promised myself that my career would be my focus and romantic relationships would take a backseat. Somewhere along the line, however, romantic relationships became my priority. Breaking my promise to myself, that integrity breach, threw everything out of whack. Again, this is not about morality, so the idea is certainly not to shame or blame yourself for breaking promises. Think of it as "happened" or "didn't happen." Cold, hard fact. I didn't keep my promises to myself. Period. No judgment. We're simply inquiring into the reality of the situation.

Lastly, once you're clear on where you have breached integrity, determine how you can restore workability to that area of your life. I invite you to start accepting that current reality, not because it's always glorious perfection, but because it's all that's real. It's true. You can count on it. Yes, it can change, but what will truly release you from suffering is to welcome what it is now. The pain and suffering shows you what's left to investigate. It shows what's blocking you from making love and a constant glow your new reality. From there, you can restore integrity and create a new occurring world.

This whole "accepting what is real" thing doesn't have to be ugly and scary. This is an exciting process of revealing the light that was present all along. You can see that your journey has molded you for the greater good. You didn't waste your time. It took every situation and heartache you encountered to bring you into the right now. It was exactly what it needed to be, and now is right on time. When you can accept and love what is, then you tap into your innate wisdom. You can see where the universe has been leading you.

When it comes to born expertise, many of us are like fish swimming in water. We're so acclimated to our environment, to the knowledge that buoys us, that we don't even notice it. If you're a yoga teacher, then other yoga teachers and students who know a lot of similar information likely surround you. You forget that most of the world does not possess this expertise. Consider this: you could be taking your genius for granted. You know stuff, like *know* in your muscles, that other people don't know. And when you know stuff that other people do not, you're in a position to be of service. Then, imagine if you're being of service with something that feeds your spirit—you could serve and LOVE doing it. Sounds glowy and fabulous to me!

How do you use what you've got to advance your worldly ambition? More specifically, how do you stand out among all the like-minded geniuses you surround yourself with? You leverage what you already know with what turns you on. Ask, *What business are you really in?*

Ray Kroc, the founder of McDonald's, asked a class of MBAs what business they thought he was in. *"Restaurants. Food. Hamburgers,"* they answered, predictably. Nope! Ray Kroc explained,

> *Real estate. The success of McDonalds was based on putting restaurants in as many locations as possible. The empire wasn't so much about the Big Mac as it was about giving people easy access to the Big Mac. Location, location, location.*

You may be an event planner who is really in the business of stress management; a hair stylist who doubles as a therapist; a receptionist as a creative bodyguard. Yoga studios are more than centers for weird contortions: they're community builders. Danielle LaPorte reflects, *"I'm in the wisdom-broadcasting business. I convert information into knowledge, give it my personal perspective, and then deliver it in every format possible. I either give it away for free or sell it."* Me? I'm in the inspiration business. I convert human behavior to patterns, give it my own flare, and then empower people to empower themselves.

Ask yourself: *What is the experience I'm giving to people? Who needs me the most? What do I do for them that affects their life or their work even for a moment?* Assuming that you're speaking from your own voice, you bring a particular slant or paradigm to what you're talking about. That creates an experience for people: they get empowered to act, the facts sober them up, and the beauty melts them. What do you love knowing about? The NBA, lawnmowers, nail polish, roasting coffee? What is it that you want people to know, see, or understand? Your life is your message to the world. Make sure it's what you really want to say. Get creative! What are your methods of expression? I express through writing, talking, and movement. *"When I say creative,"* the writer, Osho, illustrates, *"I don't mean you should all go and become great painters and great poets. I simply mean let your life be a painting, let your life be a poem."* Every single one of us is an artist at something: legal persuasion, medicine, or graphic design. You become closer to the world and yourself when you do your art.

Your curiosity is your starting point. Get better at what you're best at. When you deepen your interests and stretch your talents, the world feels bigger and full of promise. You'll see more and make connections with the greater whole. Aspiring to something greater makes you more accessible, more vulnerable, and that's where the learning happens. When do you feel amazing? When does your muse visit you? Passion will move you in the direction of your authentic self. When someone is integrated with what's real, she shows up: not because she is compelled to, but because she can hardly resist. She asks really good questions, because she is always scanning for the right fit. She gets really comfortable saying no to things that pull her away from what she is here to do. She is incredibly generous. She looks you in the eye.

> *"When you've tapped into your innate genius, the universe lovingly guides you to uncover it further."*

Where do you find enthusiasm? The root term "entheos" means having the universe within, which pulls in what we've discussed about genius: your enthusiasm is innate. Before you commit, take the stage, take the meeting, or take your place in the intentional unfolding of your life, enthusiasm—connection to what is, universe and all—must be present. This is bright faith in reality. It's not the grounding, assurance/insurance type of faith. It's the insanely ripe with potential enthusiasm that happens with new ideas. When you've tapped into your innate genius, the universe lovingly guides you to uncover it further.

You have this passion and innate wisdom, whether you've found it or not, and you're being guided to reveal it. This means you must get vulnerable for the sake of your purpose, your authentic genius. We're back to the inquiry and interpretation process: Are you resisting the guidance that the universe is providing? You know those big, juicy dreams you have swirling around in your head and heart? I'm talking helping thousands, meeting your soul mate, traveling for a living, starting a flourishing family or business. Receiving these miracles requires you to be the highest, most-uncovered version of yourself.

Don't get me wrong—you don't need to become someone else. Quite the opposite. The highest version of you, the glowing you, is there, perhaps deep down, underneath the layers of self-hate, fear, and limiting beliefs. This is about peeling down the layers. When you want things, the universe wants them too. We *all* benefit when you're the most abundant version of you. In fact, the universe is going to step up to make this version of you a reality.

Here's the rub: when you want more, you must grow more, which means you'll be given more and harder challenges. When you start this exploration of glow, you have all kinds of expectations. You're looking for solutions to that hunger, that emptiness that's been present for years. The last thing you expect is further introduction to fear. The highest version of you is about knowing fear, knowing that it is what it is. Looking it right in the eye, not as a way to solve problems, but as an undoing of old ways of seeing, hearing, thinking, feeling, smelling, and living. With every challenge, you are humbled by fear, so that your strength and courage must grow. As a glow-getter, life is constantly in transition. We will go from one hurdle to the next. If you want all these big, juicy dreams, get ready to meet the next challenge, instead of dreading it.

I remember when my spectacular 22-year-old friend Cameron was about to embark on a six-month hike through the Appalachian Mountains, alone, with no money other than the $1,000 she raised from an Indiegogo campaign. She was panicking. Now you can criticize or revere this journey, but we can agree on one thing: Cam is ballsy. She had the *chutzpah* to look fear in the face every step of the way—she found the trail; she committed to doing this nutty thing alone; she organized the Indiegogo campaign. She dared greatly before she even set out on the hike. Why? Because she had a clear purpose: come right back to herself, to look fear in the eye and see its kindness. Her journey reminds us all of fear's beauty. It's pointing us in the direction of where we are hidden beyond the shame, blame, and judgments. The crazy experience of the hike aside, she began revealing the kind of person she was before she even left the house.

In the revealing, in the depth and honesty in approaching challenges, your vulnerability is the most beautiful tool you have. "What if I bare all and people think I'm weak, stupid, or a fraud?" you may say. This is shame. While guilt says, "I did something wrong," shame in all of its self-destructiveness says, "I am wrong." When the fear points you back to yourself, you learn to love yourself, not in the, "I'm better than you" kind-of way, but in the "We've all got our big-ugly tails" kind-of way. The result of this vulnerability allows leadership, connection, and accomplishment.

It's not about competition. It's about adding to the progress of the world. When you stop competing and start celebrating your bare-all reality, you learn to love the process. You can love what is real right now. When you identify with a painful circumstance and make it a personal affront, the result is self-destruction. When you make that journey from "I'm flawed" to "I am enough, right now, as I am," you actually learn to love the difficult times. Recognize that we all experience shame. By realizing the ridiculous effort to hide it, self-hate can get quieter and quieter and soon turn into a compliment.

All that's left are imperfections: be the five-year old you that eats potato chips on your bedroom floor and calls cute boys. The girl without the shame. In Cam's case, there was no room to get away from that person, no exit, no drugs, no phones... nowhere to run. When fear's sting turns into a loving embrace, you see what you see. You feel what you feel, and from that you connect with the innate genius that is always present.

At the end of Eat Pray Love, Elizabeth Gilbert names this hunger, "The Physics of the Quest." She describes,

> If you're brave enough to leave behind everything familiar and comforting, which can be anything from your house to your bitter, old resentments, and set out on a truth-seeking journey, either internally or externally, and if you're willing to regard everything that happens to you on that journey as a clue and accept everyone you meet along the way as a teacher and if you are prepared, most of all, to face and forgive some very difficult realties about yourself, then the truth will not be withheld from you.

Your decision to raise your consciousness, your hunger for a successful, satiating life, will lead you home. You will find your purpose: to uncover, be, and love your authentic self. You can give up on trying to be perfect or better than the next person. Instead, when you "face and forgive some very difficult realities" about yourself, you can experience what it's like to live in the beauty that already is present. Then, and only then, can you move towards your potential...

You are the glow, and after an entire book about cultivating this shine, we're now ready to dive into your effect. The effect, your vision of progress, is how you move and transform your world. Do you move people to help create your vision, or do you compel them to run the other direction? When you have a vision that others can align with, whether it's advocacy for the wealthy or going on a lone trek through the wilderness to gain insight into the self, you will move people. You may move people to bring you assistance or simply inspire them to get their own *tuchus* into gear. While you cultivate your glow, you will no doubt magnetize like-minded people and inspire your outer world.

My guess is that there is something specific you want to create, and like I promised, there is The Glow Effect way of creating it. Clearly, The Glow Effect is not about manipulation. Intimately related to accepting what is real is accessing your potential, creating results through inspiration. With inspiration you don't have to convince or force people to act. People move from their own impetus. To move into potential and inspire others, The Glow Effect requires three elements: (1) clarify your effect, (2) know how to create it, and (3) get out of your own way.

WHAT WILL BE YOUR EFFECT?

In order to have an effect, you must know what you want your effect to be. What exactly do you want to create? Before we can discuss how to move people, you must know where and why you're moving them. By traditional definitions you can box yourself into the terms "lawyer," "yoga teacher," or "marketing consultant," but once you begin to realize your potential, you know that's only a snippet of who you are. What's the point of conducting the business that you're in? Is it guidance, assistance, advocacy, or teaching? What's the point of you revealing and augmenting more light? Why do you bother doing what you're doing on a personal and professional level? When you can answer these questions, you'll begin your glow effect.

This is the question Simon Sinek says revolutionized Apple over Dell. While Dell started with the *"What?"* and *"How?"* of their products, Apple asked *"Why?"* The difference meant venturing beyond computers to iPads, iPods, and iPhones, whereas Dell was pigeonholed as a computer company. *"By 'why' I mean your purpose, cause or belief,"* Sinek says, *"WHY does your company exist? WHY do you get out of bed every morning? And WHY should anyone care?"* This is your personal and professional mission statement. It's not just the values you've discovered from Part Two that will create results. It is turning your values into a vision and clarity about how to be, in order to move you forward from reality into possibility.

Sinek describes,

> For values or guiding principles to be truly effective they have to be verbs... It's not "innovation," it's "look at the problem from a different angle." Articulating our values as verbs gives us a clear idea—we have a clear idea of how to act in any situation.

In short, if you come up with a big enough *why* to do something, you will figure out the *how* to achieve it. If you want to create a massive effect, know your why first—dream of the effects, the ripples, and the joy. Up your dreams and refine them. If your current reality is nowhere close to the life you want, visioning is the fuel that will move you forward. If you want to access your full range of glow power, then commit to figuring out your vision.

Creating your effect is based on a decision to bring whatever you want into being. You need not know how, you just know that you must.

Remember, it's not the events that shape your life and determine how you feel and act, but, rather, it's the way you *interpret* and *evaluate* life experiences. Since possibilities are endless, it's up to you to consciously choose an empowering interpretation. There is no way you should act, be, or feel. All of these will come out of the story that you choose.

In one situation, a boyfriend told me, *"I no longer wanted to date you."* That's what happened. Fact. How I interpreted that situation wasn't real. It was simply one perspective of the event. In other words, what did I take those words to mean? I heard that I'm not enough—pretty, smart, confident, generous, and every other enough. I decided that I would change my disempowering 'enough' story. All I needed was another possible perspective: It was possible that this breakup had absolutely nothing to do with me being enough and had everything to do with us not being right for one another. Therefore, it was possible that this event was an awesome blessing, strengthening and preparing me for a better partner. Is the blessing possibility truer than my enough interpretation? Perhaps, but that's irrelevant. I invented the possibility, and I decide in every moment what potential I want to experience.

You're constantly making evaluations for what things mean and what you should do. Thus, if you want different results, transform the questions to get better answers. If you ask, "Why does this always happen to me?" Your mind will come up with an answer. If you are struggling to lose weight, it's not that you can't. It's that you're not asking the right questions. Rather than, "What would make me feel the most full? Or what foods can I get away with?" Ask: *What would really nourish my vessel? What's light and can give me energy?* Instead of affirmations, ask, *What am I happy about now? What could I be happy about if I wanted to?* If you're starting a business, ask, *What's the worst thing that can happen, and can I handle it?* And perhaps, *What's the best possible outcome, and is it worth the risk?* Questions get your mind to work a different way.

The questions will show you where you need to build a healthy foundation. By being solution-oriented and always improving, you have nothing to fear. Your brain will search for empowering alternatives to your difficulties. You will refine your vision and suddenly have the answers to make it come into being. You will create new habits, standards, and expectations that will help you expand.

The WHY is the first step, then decide what will effectuate that vision. Though I have a vision of women's empowerment, and I create that through books and training, you may choose to empower through teaching spin classes. But that's only the beginning... What do you hope to attain through each spin class? What's the next step in building your classes? Where do you see the classes going? Do you want to open your own spin studio? Why? The point is that when you have clear goals, then you have purpose: you know the what to get to your why. Goals are merely dreams with deadlines.

When I quit my job, I had a general sense of what I was good at and what I wanted to do. I had chiseled away divorce law as an option—not part of my master plan. Then, I did this exercise that created a future so compelling that it changed my life. I established what I was committed to creating in my life. I set aside my limiting beliefs and journaled every possibility I could imagine doing, being, creating, experiencing, and contributing. There were no thoughts of whether I could accomplish any of these things. I embodied that childish dreamer. Then, I collected all of my long-term goals for my mental, spiritual, emotional, physical, and financial futures and created a series of milestones working backwards. I asked, *If I want to achieve my top mental goals fives years from now, what kind of person do I have to be and what do I need to accomplish? Most importantly, what specific action could I take today that would lead me to this future?*

I ask you, what do you want for your life if you could have anything you want? What would you go for if you knew you couldn't fail?

_____

_____

_____

_____

Don't get caught up with the details, like what kind of flowers you want in your garden. Just say, "I want a garden." Then, figure out how you want to feel. Remember, feelings are the symbols for an emotional experience. Imagine what it would feel like to master or attain these things.

How would you feel about yourself? Your life?

_____

_____

_____

_____

Put these goals somewhere where you will see them daily. Look at these mental, spiritual, emotional, physical, and financial goals while you commute, brush your teeth, and take off your makeup. Twice a day, create the emotional experience you will have by achieving these goals.

By looking at these goals, you will condition your nervous systems to create new beliefs, new associations for what will bring you pleasure and pain. When you imagine the excitement, connection, or love that you can experience, you'll create a neural pathway between what is real and your potential. Then, with this intense conditioning, you'll create a sense of absolute certainty of achieving your dreams. You won't visualize possibility as future—you'll visualize possibility as right now.

HOW WILL YOUR EFFECT COME TO BE?

Your effect—the movement into your vision—doesn't have the option for failure. In fact, there is no such thing as failure: only results. Do you feel your success and ideal life emerging or starting to come into view?

Good, because it's already there. As I've mentioned before, while your glow was present all along, your effect was trailing along too. It has to be, because your glow effect is linked to your growth. As you grow and glow, you move your world. The movement you create is what attracts resources, support, and people who need you. In metaphysical terms, you think it and so it is. If your conviction for your effect is strong and consistent enough, there is no question whether it will come to be: it already is. The key is to match your vibration with the vibration of whatever it is you desire. You have to be and communicate the change that you want to see in the world.

Begin by enlisting others in your new way of being, in the vision. When I say "enroll" I don't mean registering someone in a program. I mean causing a new possibility to be present for another so they're touched, moved, and inspired by that possibility. When you completely distinguish the possibility you want to create, if it's authentic, clear, and genuine, then it's inspiring to you. When it's inspiring to you, then it's inspiring to others. No effort is required to transform how others see you and what you're creating. Inspiration grounded in possibility is naturally contagious: everyone gets it and everyone wants it. Your vision literally enrolls others by itself.

When I took responsibility for my own transformation, I had to master the delivery of who I really am and who I want to be. (Otherwise, the world would deliver what it expects of me.) The delivery of a new possibility is a transformed conversation. That kind of conversation begins by getting the ego out of the way and entering the world of spirit consciousness. In other words, communicating from the level of community connection rather than self. This requires restoring integrity: acknowledging broken promises and the impact of those breaks. Taking responsibility for reality disappears any egotism.

As an example, I told my mother, my closest friend and confidant, about my promise to myself that I'd be driven and focused on my business, but instead I'd been dramatic and obsessing over guys. The impact of that broken promise was self-doubt and anger towards everyone around me. By restoring integrity, I got vulnerable, shocking the ego. My mom was able to see this situation distinct from me and reflected on the possibility of this kind of change in her own life. From there, we saw a clearing: egos disappeared and a space for creation remained. We filled that space with a new possibility. I delivered what I saw possible for my life when I became the person I want to be. She created the possibility for her own life. We participated in each other's visions as well: *"Please communicate with me when you see me not being that. I will do the same for you."* We were both enrolled in a new reality.

A transformed conversation isn't persuasion into your new way of being. It isn't coercion. This kind of force may accomplish something by temporarily altering a person's behavior, but that's not transformation. It's not transformation when the power stays with the persuader, with the coercer. If it's really transformation, the listener gets the power. This transformed conversation is creating a new possibility for another so they're touched, moved, and inspired to see you and the object of the discussion in a new way. Her action towards you and that object then comes from within. In being touched, moved, and inspired, the listener discovers her own access to power, freedom, and glow. This is your glow effect coming into reality through others.

Start by evaluating which people you need to enroll to make your vision a reality. Who is already earning the amount you want to earn, loving the way you want to love, or doing what you want to do? What skills do you need? Who do you need to call, email, or potentially even cut out of your life to make these things possible? Never leave the site of setting a goal without first taking a positive action toward its attainment. And then get ready to set more goals. How many people do you know who meet their goals only to say, "Is this all there is?" You need to continually create compelling goals to grow.

When The Glow Effect began, there was no doubt in my mind that all its possibility would come to be. I knew it already existed somewhere out there. I knew I would be shown the teachers, tools, and glow-getters that would join me in moving others. The journey to bring it into being through my delivery of the vision was the whole point. I held the vision and the knowing of its existence, but I released the forcing. I just kept having conversations. My first workshop had one person. The second had a few more. With every step, I learned more, grew more and refined the vision more. There was no "finally" when I reached a goal, because I envisioned and shared more goals. I got stronger and more courageous with each step. The universe provided the resources, teachers, and support the whole time. My job was to enroll whomever came into my path.

When you're attracting and manifesting your vision, then you can use Joseph Campbell's most famous advice, *"follow your bliss."* In the PBS series, Campbell replied to a Moyers question about whether "hidden hands" guide and facilitate our work once we've found our path:

> *All the time. It is miraculous. I even have a superstition that has grown on me as a result of invisible hands coming all the time— namely, that if you do follow your bliss you put yourself on a kind of track that has been there all the while, waiting for you, and the life that you ought to be living is the one you are living. When you can see that, you begin to meet people who are in your field of bliss, and they open doors to you. I say, follow your bliss and don't be afraid, and doors will open where you didn't know they were going to be.*

Following your bliss will lead you to the life that has been awaiting you, the path that's been there all along. When you reach this point, opportunities and connections materialize, because this is the path you are meant to follow. This doesn't have to be a spiritual concept. It's vibration: it's a current of energy that runs through our universe pushing us towards progress and growth. When you step into the current, not only will you be empowered, the world will receive the benefits of your genius.

What emerges is a very capitalist-seeming, economic principle coined by Adam Smith in the 18th century, called the "invisible hand theory." According to the invisible hand theory, each of us, acting in our own self-interests, generates a demand for goods and services that compels others to deliver those goods and services in the most efficient manner. Although economists broadly accept this theory to explain the forces of a free market, the hope is that focusing on your highest self raises the good of all. In contrast to a process that relies on individual force alone, when each person is fulfilling their purpose most effectively, resources are allocated in the most efficient manner. Economics aside, this is not a call for selfishness, but an appeal for self-love. When you're focused on your purpose and affecting your genius (interior design, loving your family, teaching Sunday school, et al) then the world will benefit. The issue with the capitalist bend is that we can't rely solely on the trickle-down effect. We must first be clear on the global "why" before we reap the benefits.

The invisible hand theory says that not only will the world rise up from your genius but also that the world will help you get there. Invisible hands come in to guide, support, and even break you down so that you may breakthrough to the next level of your glow. In 1958, Economist Leonard Read wrote an essay in the first-person perspective of a pencil:

> *I, Pencil, the creation of a pencil am a complex combination of miracles: a tree, zinc, copper, graphite and so on. But to these miracles which manifest themselves in Nature an even more extraordinary miracle has been added: the configuration of creative human energies—millions of tiny know-hows configuring naturally and spontaneously in response to human necessity and desire, all in the absence of any human masterminding!*

Miraculously, humans respond to need and desire by collaborating our creativities to grow the world. Nature is this current through which you either align for power or refuse in favor of human force. When we humans get creative, we tap into nature. Thus, the answer as to how your effect will come to be is simple: leave the human masterminding out of the equation. It gets in the way. Move yourself towards glow through transformative conversations: get your ego out of the way and create the new possibility for another.

Get creative. Tap into your genius. Get clear on your purpose, and surrender into alignment with this innate, universal power. Then share it.

Let me be clear: being salesy and pushy for the bling and the bucks is not what will create a glow effect. A glow effect will organically emerge when restoring integrity brings down people's walls. People are being bombarded with sales messages an average of 62.1 times a day. We are being inundated with choices. The average person receives more information on a daily basis than an average person received in a lifetime in 1900. Hence, people have put up walls to limit stimuli. According to Dr. Robert S. Hartman, PhD, on average, people hold back 40% of their cooperation and productivity. That means they put up a wall, and you only get 60% of them. It's closer to an 80% wall when they are being sold, recruited and directed. That means you get 20% of a person. Instead of selling, share your humanness, restore your integrity and look for their good; not in appearance but in innate value, like compassion, persistence, confidence or joy. Notably, we don't bring down walls to manipulate, exploit, or take advantage of vulnerability. It is a privilege to see behind the walls. Be mindful as you use such availability to create your movement towards transformation.

I often get the question, *"How long does it take until I get _____ (fill in: success, glow, my ideal life)?"* The answer: until you get results. You can accomplish anything with what I call the "VACA Formula": Vision, massive Action, Catching things that are off, and Adjusting accordingly. The term vaca actually means cow in Spanish. In Hinduism, cows symbolize the connectedness of all creatures, the Earth, the nourisher, and the ever-giving, undemanding provider. It represents the sustenance of life, taking nothing but water, grass and grain. It gives and gives and gives of its milk and its meat, as the liberated soul gives of his spiritual knowledge. So too, when you tap into your genius and discover the why to create, your daily work is to build and deliver that vision to the world. This doesn't mean backbreaking work. This means surrendering to guidance, allowing the universe to tell you when to rest, when to connect, and when to build. The VACA Formula is a co-creation formula where the universe will provide what you need to correct your course and create results. This is how you know that a delay in your vision is not a denial. It is simply a message to redirect your path. You must be willing and available to listen. Then, you share and share and try and try until you create your effect.

Getting a "no" from someone or something that you want is part of a larger yes from the universe, though you can't always see it. The key is to interpret rejection of the "yes" as grace. You are being groomed, prepared and polished so that when you do create a glow effect, you have not only the capacity to see that this is what you've been asking for, but also the courage and humility to receive it. If all your inner blocks were removed, you would be able to receive your effect now. But more often you have so much internal resistance that you keep the good out. Detach from the form it comes in and be receptive to the subtle messages and guidance you receive daily. Choose to interpret rejection as grace, instead of the end of the world. As the poet Rumi says, *"If you're bothered by every rub, how will you ever be polished?"*

YOU'RE GLOWING AND GROWING—GET OUT OF THE WAY!

Having this dream-like success is about taking a big leap towards your zone of glowing genius. You must foster the mental, spiritual, and physical muscles to receive and hold your vision. No one can save you or do it for you. Ultimately, you must be the hero of your own life. You must create the change you want to see in the world by being, communicating and living your vision. This comes back to having conversations of possibility, like I mentioned above. This shift in understanding is difficult: you are taught that you must earn, achieve, and accomplish in order to be loved. But this is not so: you're already loved. You're already powerful and glowing. You simply need to peel back the layers limiting your light and effect. You need to bust through the blocks to let the good in. You need to enroll others in your new possibility.

Marianne Williamson says it best: *"Our deepest fear is not that we are inadequate. Our deepest fear is that we are powerful beyond measure. It is our Light, not our Darkness, that most frightens us."* Often attributed to Nelson Mandela, who used it in his 1994 inaugural address to enroll South Africans in a new possibility, this quote sums up your own barriers to living with glow. Every suffering, from anger to disappointment, can be pinned on the fear of your glow effect. The consequence of such fear? You block your greatness. You block your light.

"When you tap into limitless abundance you already are, there is enough money, love and freedom to go around"

Being "powerful beyond measure" does not mean that you're better, more capable, or smarter than anyone else. Each and every one of us has the capacity for greatness. Power manifests through connecting, loving and consistently giving. The second you compare, hoard and constrict, you limit your capacity and power. When you tap into the limitless abundance you already are, there is enough money, love and freedom to go around. Like Williamson says, the issue is not of your adequacy to achieve your greatness, the issue is whether you can allow yourself to realize your immense light.

I've read this quote countless times over the past ten years, thinking, *Well, isn't that lovely—I'm powerful.* I never fully appreciated the concept until I became conscious of my effect. For those years of mindlessly reading this quote, I identified as small. Unknowingly, I held myself back as undeserving of power. This quote spoke to a subtle voice that kept whispering, You're more than that. Over the past years since I've been exploring my genius, that voice has grown so loud that when I act in contradiction, the repercussions include sadness, anger, exhaustion and sickness. An identity crisis emerged: *Am I small or powerful? Wealthy or poor? A lawyer or a teacher? Worthy or unworthy? A Chicagoan, Pittsburgher, New Yorker, Californian, free bird? Loving or selfish?* The answer is that I'm all of the above. I'm anything I want to be. This is my fear of power. I move forward by employing the "fake-it-till-I-make-it" technique, i.e. pretending I am powerful until I actually feel powerful. Beautifully, my light attracts more light. People with incredible knowledge come out of woodwork, and I discover skills that I didn't even know I possessed. In other words, identity is not tied to words, money, people or places. You are all of this and so much more than your little mind can grasp. You invent what you want to be in every moment; enlisting yourself and others in the vision makes it real.

You are powerful beyond measure.

On the other side of the spectrum, as you navigate through this identity crisis and realize the immensity of your glow, self-protection manifests. This is the *Upper Limit Problem (ULP)*, as defined by psychologist, Gay Hendricks. In short, you have a glass ceiling of yummy feelings that you impose on yourself, and then create behavior to prevent yourself from feeling any better. Everyone has an inner thermostat of how happy we allow ourselves to be. If you were any happier, there's a part of you that thinks you'll die. Some people refer to this as "self-sabotage," but you're not consciously sabotaging yourself. You're protecting yourself. Indeed, you must protect yourself from daily risks to survive crossing the street, squandering cash, eating entire jars of peanut butter and all of life's other great risks. However, when protection becomes excessive, you suppress your power.

Sometimes, when I witness my business-baby growing, my ULP kicks in. I used to react with, *This is the limit of my greatness. I can't hold such joy.* (Hands shielding my face while in a fetal position). When I stretched out, literally and figuratively, I found that protection was unnecessary: the glass ceiling is an illusion. Thus, while you need to realize your greatness identity, you also need to push past your protective instincts. It is outside of that protective, comfort zone where your true glow effect lives.

I like to call work with ULP, "The Weed Diet." Your ultimate success and ideal life, the effects of your glow, mean to continually cultivate an abundant garden of possibility. Weeds are the integrity breaches of the deepest, most harmful kind. Weeds occur when you have these compelling goals and you diminish yourself with certain thoughts and actions, breaking the promises you make with yourself. The five integrity breaches include worry, criticism and blame, deflection, arguments, and sickness.

Things going well triggers the ULP, and you worry about things going wrong in some way. You justify those worry thoughts with more worry thoughts, which spirals into an overall doom scenario. There are two questions to ask as to whether your worry thought is something you should pay attention to: (1) Is it a real possibility? and (2) Is there any action I can take right now to make a positive difference? Often the thought is a prevention of another healthy, powerful thought, and when you're attached to it, you're thrown off your power. Notice the worry thoughts, and choose to not attach to them. Notice what positive thing is trying to come up, and then try to sink into that sensation. For example, when you get a raise, you get greedy and increase your expenses, which brings back your worry about money. Instead of thinking that you're actually worried about money, see that these thoughts are ULP symptoms. Rarely do these thoughts have anything to do with reality.

With criticism and blame towards yourself and others, you're trying to halt the flow of power, genius and success. The blame game is highly addictive and rarely useful. If you're curious to test the criticism addiction, try to go 24 hours without criticizing or blaming. If it's not an addiction you'll be able to stop right away. Two things to note in criticism and blame: (1) you've come out of spirit consciousness—you've stopped seeing that everyone (and/or you) is trying to achieve their version of pleasure and avoid their version of pain, and (2) you made a decision in the situation, whether creating the cause or the interpretation, so, in that way, you've chosen this reality. Start to notice all the criticisms about real things ("You're on my toe") versus the projections of fault ("Your behavior is awful"). Take responsibility for the things that you can change.

Perhaps you prohibit your success by avoiding it all together. Think of how many compliments you stifle. Deflection keeps you from receiving positive energy. You need it, and the person giving it needs you to receive it. Again, *A Course in Miracles* defines this giving and receiving as one truth. The art of creating a continuous glow effect, going beyond the ULP, is about creating space within to feel and appreciate naturally good feelings. By extending this ability, you expand your tolerance for things going well in your life.

Arguments, or squabbling, are another way to bring yourself away from your glow effect. First, understand why arguments occur. Arguments are caused by two people/countries/factions racing to occupy the victim position. Person A claims the victim position ("Why are you doing this to me?") and then tries to get person B to agree with that assessment. Per the nature of argument, person B has to agree that she is the persecutor. Therein lies the problem. It's almost impossible to get the other party to agree that it's her fault. For your glow effect, you cannot be an island. You must approach relationships by taking full responsibility for resolving conflict. Ideally, the other person will also approach with full responsibility, so there is total commitment. The fatal flaw is thinking there is a total of one hundred percent responsibility in any relationship. This is ego consciousness:

fifty percent per person. In such limited consciousness, you're vying for the victim position when apportioning the hundred percent. Spirit consciousness, in contrast, gives each party one hundred percent responsibility. There is no such thing as blame: the decision to stay whole allows the utmost effect.

Another pattern we employ to cut off glowing genius is sickness and getting hurt. Think of the times you've gotten sick or hurt and whether these have happened when things are going well. I'm not saying that every instance is an ULP symptom, but it helps to see sickness and hurt as potential symptoms. When I was an attorney, I would get a different ailment every week: one week the flu, the next a neck spasm, the following an awful cold. I now see that I was unconsciously preventing my joy. As we speak, I haven't been sick or hurt in almost 2 years. The three Ps help you understand the driving force behind many illnesses and accidents: punishment, prevention, and protection. You can punish yourself for awesome feelings with migraines, nausea, the flu, or colds. Prevention and protection often go together when you're unconsciously trying to protect yourself from something you don't want to do or feel. In my case, I didn't want to be in my job.

Often there are positive messages and powerful calls to action just underneath the surface of all "negative" symptoms and emotions. The bottom line: you don't have to feel bad about weeds in the glow garden. Acknowledge them, focus on the solution, and immediately do whatever it takes to eliminate their influence on your life.

Here's what's important to get: at the level of ego consciousness, all of these reasons to proceed are valid and convincing. Abandoning your work towards your glow effect makes sense. At the level of spirit, in contrast, there are few reasons more important than fulfilling your purpose. When you know your Why, How, and substance of moving people, you can create an effect of massive proportions. It's up to you to hold those proportions with grace and glow. It's time to take action and build your vision.

CONCLUSION | YOUR GLOW IS SHOWING

If you have retained one thing, and one thing only, I hope it's this: it's your light that lights the world. Just as every vote counts in a democracy, every person is contributing to the light of the world. Your light is either bright or it is dimmed. It's either manifesting your vision for world change or draining the unique gifts only you can provide.

In order to create a glow effect, your consciousness and habits, stories and relationships, and reality and potential must be working together to grow your glow sphere. Always begin with yourself. Again and again come back to you at the center of the circle. Be the hero of your own life.

Of course, this isn't easy. Pray not for an easy life, but the strength to endure a challenging one. The life of a glow-getter is just that: challenge. It must be, for you're constantly growing in order to hold your glow effect of massive proportions.

Let it be emphasized, however, you are not alone. You're never alone. You're deeply connected to life and power. When you begin to see the light in others, and inspire rather than manipulate their movement, you'll have the support and love you need to endure.

Believe in your light.
Believe in your strength.
Be the change.

Be The Glow Effect.

DEDICATION

To my grandfather, Thomas Cohn, PhD.

You had the biggest ego of anyone I'll ever meet. Your ego was so big that your self-doubt kept you from sharing your wisdom on human behavior in a book and instead philandering.

Fortunately, your overly-analytical, inappropriately-philosophical and annoyingly-challenging character was passed to me. So my dearest Pa, this is the book you never managed to write and that we both wanted to read.

I miss and love you always, Pa.

P.S. The book is meant to empower women. Wherever you are in the clouds, I hope you appreciate the irony.

Meet SAREN:

Saren is the vibrant creator of The Glow Effect
and The Glow Exchange, a nonprofit connecting
and empowering women in developed and
developing communities to build women's centers.
Though she'll forever be a Pittsburgh girl at heart,
she now lives and loves in LA. If she's not getting
vulnerable with the #glowgetter tribe, you can
find her yoga-ing or indulging in her unhealthy
addiction to green juice.

Find out more at gloweffect.com.

Made in the USA
San Bernardino, CA
13 October 2016